Reflections From the Sunrise

THE HANDIWORK OF GOD IN EVERY DAY LIFE

LAURIE GANIERE

FOR PERSONAL DEVOTIONS OR SMALL GROUP STUDY

ISBN-13: 978-1981976324
ISBN-10: 1981976329

Cover Design and Book Layout: Sarah Dams

Cover Photo: Trevor Todd (ttodd.co)

THANKS

Of course everything I do is birthed out of my relationship with Jesus. He is the one that inspires me to create. I've never thought of myself as creative until my artist, song writing son told me that what I do is create. He is right. From deep in my soul, I write. I thank my God for giving me the gift of words, humor and insight so that others are able to glean truths about Him through them. Thank you!

I thank my husband Rick for his unending hours piling through all my works, proofing everything before it goes to print. Next to Jesus you are my best friend, lover, one that can make me giggle at the corniest things, and even partner in crime. I love you!

I thank Debbie Oseland for her incredible skill in editing. You've made me think so much deeper than I thought I could. Thank you for challenging me and giving SO many hours to making my work better. You're AWESOME. Thank you!

Trevor Todd, thank you for your photography that inspired this cover. Your eye for beauty is captured in your work. I am so grateful for your generosity to allow your work to collide with mine and Sarah's, to give this dream a face. Thank you!

Sarah Dams, this could never be a reality without you. For all your work in design, layout and everything else that you do, from the bottom of my heart I thank you.

DEDICATION

This book became a reality because of my readers. So, so, so many people that read my first devotional, ***Can't See the Wind***, have begged for another devotional. So to you, my friends, with love and thankfulness, this book, ***Reflections from the Sunrise***, is dedicated to you. You know who you are. I love you to the moon and back. This is our book!

TABLE OF CONTENTS

INTRODUCTION

I have lived in the greater Milwaukee area for my entire life. I love MKE. It is my town. It is the place I enjoy riding my motorcycle and praying for so many that are lost, broken and without Jesus.

When I began looking for a photograph that was truly MKE, there were so many to choose from. So many wonderful photographers with an incredible eye for beauty in this city. Looking at some of those photos one day on a Facebook page called DearMKE, I stumbled across one by Trevor called, "Where the Sidewalk Ends." Not only did I love the photo, but I loved the title and was determined that would be the name of this book. I was able to reach Trevor who so graciously gave me permission to use his photo. Then I did a search on book titles, only to find there was already a book entitled ***Where the Sidewalk Ends.*** So, it was back to the title search to best capture why this book exists.

In my great love for MKE, comes my love for our great lake, Michigan. My husband Rick knows my favorite bridge into our city is the Hoan Bridge. The cityscape is beautiful and the lake is breathtaking.

Over the years, I have often made time to stop and just ponder life and have incredible conversations with God down at this great lake. So many times I picked up lunch or coffee from the coffee shop and just sat and had quiet time there. There have been times when God has spoken to me so clearly, usually quite simply through the reflections on "my lake in my town."

If there is a main theme in this book, it is this: God is involved in our every day lives. We often miss Him simply because we aren't looking.

So in these devotions, it is truly my prayer that you are able to see a reflection of Him too, in your every day life; that it will inspire you to really look for Him in everything. He's there. Just like the reflection of the sunrise on the water, He desires for you to see Him everywhere.

God bless you!!!!

Laurie

WALKING IN THE LIGHT

I John 1:5-10 NIV *"This is the message we have heard from him and declare to you: God is light; in him there is no darkness at all. [6] If we claim to have fellowship with him and yet walk in the darkness, we lie and do not live out the truth. [7] But if we walk in the light, as he is in the light, we have fellowship with one another, and the blood of Jesus, his Son, purifies us from all sin. [8] If we claim to be without sin, we deceive ourselves and the truth is not in us. [9] If we confess our sins, he is faithful and just and will forgive us our sins and purify us from all unrighteousness. [10] If we claim we have not sinned, we make him out to be a liar and his word is not in us."*

Light. The value and importance of light is harder to grasp than most of us think. There are those times at night, when it's dark in the house, and we just want to get to the bathroom and back again without waking up too much. So we don't turn on the light. We can do this. We know the "terrain" in our room, we truly do. We trick ourselves into thinking we're smarter and better than we really are. The whole time, our toes, if they could talk, would be saying something like: "TURN ON THE LIGHT. PLEASE TURN ON THE LIGHT." Our other body parts would be making blinking sounds like hazard lights on a car with warnings of – "PLEASE TURN ON THE LIGHT," which we ignore altogether.

Just then, we realize that someone was up before us, and left the door to the bathroom half open, instead of fully open, and BAM. We walk right into the door. Or we cut the corner too close and catch our baby toe on the dresser. After walking into that dresser, again if those toes could talk, they would say: "I TOLD YOU TO TURN ON THE LIGHT." Your head, after running into the door, "I TOLD YOU TO TURN ON THE LIGHT."

Then in response to your pain, every muscle in your body cringes, and you cover your mouth so as to not wake anyone else up in the house. All the while getting ticked at the "dumb dresser," or "stupid door," or "stupid so and so for leaving the door half open." When, truth be known, had you turned on the light, none of this would have happened.

That's how the enemy works in our life. No matter what the "darkness" is in our life, he makes sure we have enough successes, enough journeys in the darkness WITHOUT trouble that we think it will be ok. Then when we least expect it, BAM! All because we choose to walk in the darkness!

One of those reasons that John wrote this letter is to expose doctrinal and ethical error as well as exhort God's people to pursue a life of holy fellowship with God in truth and righteousness. He says that God is light, and in Him there is no darkness at all. If we claim to be His, yet walk in darkness, the truth is not in us, we are living a lie.

There's a choice there. If we choose to walk in darkness, we're living a lie and the truth is not in us. That's not popular to preach today. Our culture says that we just all need to all be ok with everyone living the life they want to live. Of course we are free to do that, but when things go wrong, do we blame God? So often people choose to walk their own way and then get ticked at God when the consequences come. They blame HIM rather than accept the consequences because of their stupid choices. All because they chose to think they were smart enough to navigate in the dark. They didn't need the light.

He desires for us to walk safely in the light. His blessing and favor is on us as we choose to walk in the light.

If you've been traveling some on the dark road, go to ***I John 1:9***: *"if we confess our sins, he is faithful and just and will forgive us our sins and purify us from all unrighteousness."* Then, turn on the lights. Walk in the light. Choose the light. You will begin to crave it. Crave means to long for, to require, to need. The more you walk in it, the more you crave it. Walk on the lighted path today!

Reflection

1. In what ways do people today claim to have fellowship with Him yet walk in darkness?

2. In your past, how have you walked in darkness even though you claimed to have fellowship with Him?

3. How did God reveal to you that you needed Him in order to walk in His light?

4. What things did you learn then that you can apply to your current situations?

5. If you are stuck with continued consequences of walking in darkness, what does verse 9 tell us to do to find forgiveness from Him?

6. Then, turn on the lights. Get in the Word of God every day. Have conversation with Him every day.

BULLIES

Luke 12:4-7 The MESSAGE Bible *"I'm speaking to you as dear friends. Don't be bluffed into silence or insincerity by the threats of religious bullies. True, they can kill you, but then what can they do? There's nothing they can do to your soul, your core being. [5] Save your fear for God, who holds your entire life — body and soul — in his hands. [6] "What's the price of two or three pet canaries? Some loose change, right? But God never overlooks a single one. [7] And he pays even greater attention to you, down to the last detail — even numbering the hairs on your head! So don't be intimidated by all this bully talk."*

We've all experienced a bully or two in our lives. Some of us hate confrontation so much that we fall prey to bullies easier than others. That fear can consume us. On the other hand, some of us want to put on boxing gloves and fight them off. Admit it, there are some of you, when you think of someone bullying you or someone you love, you are pretty sure you "can take 'em." So you put on your boxing gloves and get in the game. Still some others just freeze and hope they will go away.

Jesus had those bullies too. They were the Pharisees, the religious leaders of His day. In the verse above, He had just finished a confrontation with the Pharisees who were trying to trap Him into saying something they could take issue with. Jesus turned His attention to His disciples. This was a great teaching moment for them. He told them not to be afraid of the bullies.

According to Dictionary.com, a bully is "a blustering, quarrelsome, overbearing person who habitually badgers and intimidates smaller or weaker people." Jesus told them to not be afraid of those men. They can't do a thing to harm your soul. He said that God is the one that holds your body and soul in His hands. Fear Him!

THEN, in the next verse Jesus tells them of their worth to God, this God that they fear. It's a different kind of fear - it's a reverence, an awe. He says God is careful to look after every single canary, and that we are worth so much more than those little birds. He cares about every detail in your life. He said, "Don't be intimidated by the bully talk." Why? Because they can't do anything to you! Keep your focus on your God and His care for you. And, He knows EVERYTHING about you – even the number of hairs on your head.

Jesus dealt with more bullies than you or I could ever deal with. He knew that His Father, God, who had control over His destiny, was going to raise Him from the dead. He had every confidence that God would take care of Him. His disciples needed to know that they should not fear them either. God cared for them as much as He cared for Jesus. God would take care of them.

Rise up dear ones. Rise up to your position in Christ. Know His Word and let it sink deep in your soul to know His plans for you are good. His protection and care for you is unquestionable and unquenchable.

I once heard someone say that when a lion comes in and roars loudly that it scares the life out of whoever is around. But the loudness of the lion only means it's the oldest one. Also true of the oldest is that it has very few teeth, just the biggest roar. Can't cause you any harm, it's just scary.

Jesus sent His Spirit to live in you. Rise up in that and don't allow bullies in your life to cause you to take your eyes off of Him and the plans He has for you. Don't allow the roar of that lion to cause you to take your eyes off of whose you are. The lion feeds on fear, bullies feed on fear and only have the control that you give them. You have nothing to fear. God cares for you more than anything and will give you what you need to keep your eyes focused on Him and moving in the plans He has for you. Rise up friends. Rise up!

Reflection

1. What real life bullies are taunting you right now?

2. What kind of things are they telling you?

3. How does what they are telling you compare to God's Word?

4. God's Word says you are more important than that little canary. What does that tell you about Him? What does that tell you about you?

WORKING THE SEEDS

Ya know, sometimes God's provision includes a lot of hard work for us. We partner WITH Him and the blessings are there. But it most often includes some work on our part. Some buy in. Some measure of faith. He's not like some "sugar-daddy" that takes care of us just cuz He has it and we don't. Most often that provision means we work at and with what He provides for us.

That's quite the opposite of what some think. We live in a culture that has become more and more about give me, bring me, take me. Even as Christians, we think that when God promises to provide all our needs, that it will be a piece of cake. God gives and we receive. We'll wake up and everything we need will be right there. We don't have to do anything but just ingest it, use it, go in it, or pay bills with it.

Don't misunderstand – God DOES promise to meet all the needs of His people. We sing songs about how He is our provider. His Word repeatedly tells us that He is all that and so much more. But somehow, we get this picture that we don't have to do anything, just sit back and wait for Him to do it all.

One person told me many years ago that "some people are meant to give and some people are meant to receive." Meaning that it was his lot in life to be on the receiving end. Yikes. That's a little messed up. God invites us in to the journey with Him.

On the journey to the Promised Land, God provided the Israelites the food they needed every day. It was this thing called manna. It rained down manna every night and in the morning, before the sun came up, they had to go gather what they needed for their family. Read it in ***Exodus 16*** and ***Numbers 11***. It goes into much detail.

Every morning they had to bust a move and get out there before the sun grew hot. They gathered up what they needed for the day. Not two days, just for that day. It says it was like coriander seed. A quick overview about coriander seed: it's a hard little seed that has to be cooked down, or ground down into flour. If it is ground, it has to be used the same day, or the flavor goes away. The Word tells us that it tasted a little like honey wafers.

So every morning, after they gathered it, they had to cook it down, or grind it up in order to make some bread out of it. It was a lot of work. It was given to them, but there was labor involved. The sheer gathering of those little seeds was a huge amount of work. They were little seeds, tiny little seeds.

Sometimes I think we have a goofy picture of what it's like when God provides our needs. We think that if He provides, we just have to wait and do nothing. Consequently, we miss it. We would miss the manna today cuz we think Pepperidge Farm has a plane and will drop our bread every morning. Or that Miller, Grebe or National

Bakery (local bakeries in our area) will drive by and offload our provision for the day. We can just sit and wait. Now, there have been stories of miracles like that. Don't be mistaken. But to think that we don't have to be involved in the process is taking a whole lot for granted.

Some don't think they have to be involved in the process. God's provision most often comes through us partnering with Him. He never created us to be lazy people and Him our sugar daddy. He created us to partner with Him in everything in our lives.

There may be some today that are waiting for God to provide something they need. Don't miss it because you're waiting for Him to do it all. Get in the game. Open up your eyes and find those seeds. Yes, they have to be cooked or ground. It's hard work. His provision isn't often a money tree in your yard. But it IS often in some seeds waiting to be picked up.

His provision for our healing isn't always instantaneous. But He always promises to provide all we need in the process. (That's a whole other devotion.)

He doesn't always give us the perfect job that we're waiting for. Sometimes we have to flip burgers or some kind of other work until that opportunity comes. Sometimes He gives us an unglamorous job, a shack, or a jalopy, or whatever to live in, drive or work. It IS His provision for now. Don't miss it cuz it isn't exactly what you wanted.

Trust Him – always! But get in the game WITH Him. It's what Dr. David Jeremiah calls a Divine Cooperative - 100% God and 100% us. Divine things happen when we work with God. Every need we have is met.

God bless you friends. Keep looking for and gathering those seeds. Cook 'em down, grind them up. It's all part of the provision.

If you have a testimony about how God showed you the seeds before your eyes, and met your need, please email us and share that story.

resourcemin@gmail.com

Reflection

1. What have you been praying for God to provide for you or your family?

2. Is it possible that you may have missed some seeds?

    - If that is possible, ask Him to open your eyes to the provision that you may have missed.
    - Tell Him that you assumed the need would be met a certain way, and that you may have missed it.
    - Ask Him to forgive your ungrateful heart, all because you didn't see the blessing as you thought.
    - Ask Him to help you get to work, gathering those seeds.
    - I promise you, He will meet you at the very point of your need. Supernaturally, or naturaly through the gathering of the seeds.

WHERE'S MY SON?

A number of years ago, we stopped buying Christmas gifts for our family. We felt that investing in time with them all had a much greater value than things, so our money goes in to that now. Every year, we take a family trip someplace fun. This year, there were eighteen of us, including my cousin and his wife, Rick and I, our four adult kids and their families.

We had a blast. We all stayed at a hotel, visited several museums and fun places that all ages could enjoy. We laughed till our sides hurt. We toured many wonderful exhibits and 4-D shows and took hundreds of pictures to prove it. We walked and walked and walked. The kids spent a lot of free time in the hotel pool. We ate way too much food, including a LOT of cheese. (Wait, is there ever too much cheese?) You may have to be a Ganiere to fully understand that.

During one of those museum tours, we were eating lunch in the café. We were nearly done eating when we realized a woman had lost her son. She was screaming the child's name, and running around frantically in search of her child. As soon as it registered that this lady had lost her son in this sea of "strangers," my daughter-in-law Casey and I jumped up to assist. I stopped the mom and said, "We can help – what's the color of his clothing???" She told us, and continued screaming and running frantically. Both Casey and I took off in opposite directions, eyes pealed for this small child in a black shirt.

In a very short time, I looked across the room, and saw an incredible reunion. The deafening scream of this Momma was now silent. With mascara tears streaming down her face, she was hugging her beautiful young son (in a black shirt), with a pacifier in his mouth. The room erupted in cheers moments later.

There isn't a parent around that doesn't freeze at the thought of that being them in a public place. Oh the horror. It wasn't an hour later, we lost track of one of our own, a seven year old that wandered away in the gift shop. You know that in museums all roads lead to the gift shop, right? The moment we realized his cousin didn't have his hand, we all flew into search mode. His Momma and Daddy found him quickly, innocently looking at something in the shop. We thanked God for the quick find, and said seven year old learned a lesson as well.

Jesus told the story of the lost sheep in ***Luke 15:4-7 NLT*** *"If a man has a hundred sheep and one of them gets lost, what will he do? Won't he leave the ninety-nine others in the wilderness and go to search for the one that is lost until he finds it?* [5] *And when he has found it, he will joyfully carry it home on his shoulders.* [6] *When he arrives, he will call together his friends and neighbors, saying, 'Rejoice with me because I have found my lost sheep.'* [7] *In the same way, there is more joy in heaven over one lost sinner who repents and returns to God* *than over ninety-nine others who are righteous and haven't strayed away!"*

God's just not ok with one being lost. He leaves the rest, and goes to find the one that wandered away.

In that same way, we as parents just aren't ok if one of our kids is lost. Not physically or spiritually. Our hearts feel faint at the very thought of a loss like that.

Over the years in ministry, I've had many parents come to me to pray for their kids that are off doing their own thing, having wandered far away from God. I've told them all this: God loves your kids more than you do. That's hard to comprehend as a parent. There is NO ONE that loves my kids like me. But I have to tell you, God does. He truly does.

The fact that God isn't OK with one of them wandering off and that He will leave the ninety-nine to go after the one tells us the depth of that love.

Then the scripture tells us that there is a glorious celebration for the return of that lost one. As the group erupted in celebration when that woman at the museum was reunited with her son, I would say this to you today: If you have someone in your family that is spiritually lost, please know that God loves them even more than you do. He is going after them. He will leave the ninety-nine and go after your one.

Think of the rejoicing in heaven when that one is found. Because God's "on it," relax. He will never leave or forsake you or your lost one. The stakes are just too high. The stakes are their soul. God's on it!

The rejoicing in the café was only a tiny picture of a great reunion and celebration that will take place on that day. Peace be still - God's got this! God's on it!

Reflection

1. Who of your loved ones does your heart grieve for?

2. It does not matter what dragged them into the state of being lost, what matters is that God has not forgotten them. Knowing that He will leave the 99 and go after your one, how does that make you feel?

3. What fears do you still battle with? What can you do today to begin to trust the great truth of the Bible to know that He loves them more than you?

4. What scriptures can you use as a reminder to every day, every fear, every worry, turn it over to Him?

Prayer:
Father God, we know You're a big God. We know You love our loved ones even more than we do. That's inconceivable to us. But we trust that it is true based on Your Word. In faith, believing, we stand on the truth today that You are leaving the 99 to go after the one. You will send people their way to give them truth. You will speak to them in the darkness of night, when they are living in fear of their future. You will find them when they don't even want to be found. You will speak to them through things that we can only imagine that will touch their hearts with your great love, grace and mercy. You will rescue them in the same way You rescued us. Help us to trust that every day. Help us to rest in that truth every moment of every day. We look forward to the day of rejoicing and already in our hearts are planning the party. Thank you Father! Amen.

A CULTURE OF OFFENSE

One night, following Wednesday night Bible Study at our church, we stopped at a great fro-yo place near our home, owned by some good friends, who are Christians by the way. As we were enjoying our tasty treat, the owner sat down to talk with us, as usual. We normally have some giggles and talk about motorcycles, Bible School and family stuff.

That Wednesday night, our friend told us about how a woman came in to the shop and was totally offended that he was playing Christian music. She was so offended that she went back to his office to share her disgust that she had to listen to Christian music and she hated it! How dare he play Christian music in his establishment?

Our friend was way more gracious than I would have been. I believe our friend showed Jesus to her in a way that I wish I could say I would have. He was gracious, kind and caring.

As we all know, we live in a time in our country's history where everyone is offended by something. You offend me and I offend you. We spend a great deal of time bantering back and forth because we're offended by something someone said, did or thought. And we don't think twice about telling each other that we are offended and expect others to correct what we think is wrong.

As Christians, we speak about turning the other cheek. We need to learn how to shake it off, right? We are even told that it is we as Christians that cause much of the offense and that we need to get over it and make room for everyone else's rights, regardless of our own belief system.

It would appear that as Christians we are to be tolerant of everyone, but no one has to be tolerant of us. That's just the way it seems on this side of the fence. Before you pick up that offense, let's talk about this.

Offense – I believe that if and how we take offense depends largely on how we see Jesus. Do we see Him as the one who shook His finger in people's faces for how they offended Him? Was He the one that was angry with everyone for not believing or acting right? If you think so, think again. The people He got angry with were the religious leaders of the day, the Pharisees, who were critical of everything and everyone, not those that did not yet believe. The Pharisees had no grace, mercy or love for anyone. Those were the ones Jesus chastised. Those were the ones He challenged.

As for regular folks, He came to seek and to save those that were lost and broken. If you had needs, Jesus was the guy you wanted to be with. If you were hungry, physically or spiritually, He was the guy to find. If you were sick or hurt, He was the guy you wanted to be around. Something about Jesus that was so cool and captivating was that throngs of people wanted to be around Him. That's true even today.

As Christians, we have to ask ourselves, do I represent that Jesus?

There's a good reason why I'm not quoting any scriptures, I want you to go and read it for yourself. Pick a Gospel in the Bible – ***Matthew, Mark, Luke*** or ***John***. Seriously read it. If you want a clear picture of who Jesus was, read it with an open mind and heart. See clearly whom it was that He showed grace and mercy to. See for yourself who He rose against in anger. You may be surprised.

So if you're a Christian that goes around looking for stuff that offends you, shaming people and criticizing folks, you are not representing Him truthfully. Shame on you! Nobody wants to be around someone that they can never please or is constantly looking for their faults. Might you be like the religious leaders of that day? If that makes you stiffen up inside, don't shake it off. Seek Him and let Him make some changes in you. If you see Jesus that way, you are totally missing His grace, mercy and love and you may be treating others like the Pharisees did.

If you're not a Christian, and you're offended by Christians, you might ask yourself why? Why is Jesus so offensive to you? Is it because you don't know the REAL JESUS? Have you somewhere, someplace seen Christians that were like those religious leaders that Jesus came against? As a result, is that how you see all of us? If that's so, please know I will stand and apologize to you. I'm so sorry for the misrepresentation of Him that you had. Jesus isn't that. If you've been hurt by a Church or Christian somewhere in your life, please know that I believe it may have tainted your image of Jesus. He loves you and He has a great plan for your life. He came to give you life, full and free of all shame and guilt.

Pick up a Bible. Find the books of ***Matthew, Mark, Luke*** or ***John*** and read about who Jesus really was. Seriously, read it for yourself.

As Christians, we are a representation of Christ to those in our sphere of influence. Those that you work with, those in your family, in the grocery store, in your neighborhood, and even on the road when you are driving. And don't forget those in your Church family. How do they see Jesus in you? What kind of picture of the Savior are they getting from your life?

Our church gave out wristbands for us to wear following a great sermon series our Pastor did. It says, "REPRESENT." ***Colossians 3:17 NLT*** *"And whatever you do or say, do it as a representative of the Lord Jesus, giving thanks through him to God the Father."*

What are others seeing? Are we giving others a clear representation of who He is?

Reflection

1. Throughout your life, who has been a representative of God to you?

2. Because of the examples you had, what did you expect Him to be?

3. How do you see Jesus? As a disciplinarian, or a grace giving God? Explain.

4. What is a healthy representation of Him?

5. What adjustments do you need to make in yourself to better represent the Jesus of the Bible?

6. If there are others in your past that you have shown a lack of grace, mercy and love to, how will you turn that around today?

ARE YOU READY?

I Thessalonians 4:16-17 NIV *"For the Lord himself will come down from heaven, with a loud command, with the voice of the archangel and with the trumpet call of God, and the dead in Christ will rise first. After that, we who are still alive and are left will be caught up together with them in the clouds to meet the Lord in the air. And so we will be with the Lord forever."*

I Corinthians 15:51-52 NIV *"Listen, I tell you a mystery: We will not all sleep, but we will all be changed— in a flash, in the twinkling of an eye, at the last trumpet. For the trumpet will sound, the dead will be raised imperishable, and we will be changed."*

There is coming a day that we must all prepare for now. Jesus is coming back for the rapture of His Church. Those that have a relationship with Him, His people, will be caught up in the air, to be forever with the Lord. Clearly not all will be ready.

Back in the 70's, there was a series of movies about the end times, giving an incredible visual of the rapture of the church and return of Christ. The title of the first movie in

the series, "A Thief in the Night," comes from
I Thessalonians 5:2 NIV *"for you know very well that the day of the Lord will come like a thief in the night."*

Years after that series of movies, there was a 16 book series called ***Left Behind***. Those books were very popular from 1995 through 2007. There were movies made of some of these books as well.

Jesus is coming again. Just like He came the first time, He is coming again. This time, He is coming very different. He came the first time as a little baby, 100% God and 100% human. This time, He is coming to take His people home, to Heaven, to forever be with Him, and all those that have gone on before. I personally will be able to see my Mom and Dad again, and so many others in my family. I will also get to meet my twin. My Mom lost my twin while carrying us. I was born full term, but my twin was lost several months into her pregnancy. I have a twin that has already been reunited with Mom and Dad. I will meet him or her too.

Today, there are so many people that refuse to believe the truth of God's Word. There is corruption all around the world. The Bible predicted this and tells us that people would refuse to believe that God even exists. But it also tells us that God loves the world, and all the people in it, even though they don't believe in Him. That is the truth. Whether we choose to believe it or not, it doesn't change the fact that it is truth.

Further truth: Time is short, and eternity is long. Whether you believe it or not, Jesus is coming again. He is coming to take us home. The scriptures are truth. So many say the Bible is a bunch of fairy tales. Others say that our thinking that Jesus is coming to take His people home is like a sci-fi flick, that we're waiting for some kind of "mother ship" to come and take us up outta this mess. Others say there is no God. There is no life after this. My fear today is for those who don't believe there is anything after this life. Again, whether we believe it or not, doesn't change the truth that there is. God loves those people too.

He IS coming again. Some of us will be alive and leave this earth with Him in what we refer to as the Rapture of the Church. Those who are believers and have accepted Jesus Christ as their Lord and Savior will go with Him. Those who are not, will not.

The scripture tells us that there will be two people working in a field. One will be taken and one will not. Two will be sleeping in a bed and one will be taken and one will not. The one taken is the one that has a relationship with the God that saved them. The one that will be left is the one that has no relationship with God and has continually turned Him away, or denied Him. "And we KNOW NOT THE TIME OR THE DATE" when He will come, so we must be ready!

Time is short – eternity is long. We must be ready, and also make sure that our loved ones are ready too. They must make their own decisions, but we must make sure they know the truth. It's a good thing the scripture also tells us that when we are in heaven, that all our tears are no more. I can't imagine any mom or dad being there knowing that their children are not. Or that some children will be there, and their mom or dad is not. Makes my gut churn just thinking about that.

See, here's the thing. None of us is guaranteed tomorrow. I just got word today of a young man, 25 years old, healthy one day, stage 4 cancer the next. In less than 2 months, he was gone. I have a friend whose husband left for work, and 10 minutes later was in a horrible accident that claimed his life. None of us is guaranteed tomorrow. So whether it is the rapture or untimely death, are you ready?

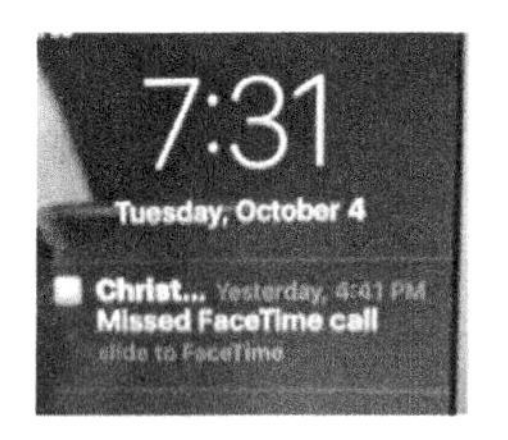

My friend Stacie posted this picture on Facebook. You can see in this post, she missed a FaceTime call from someone whose name was abbreviated as "Christ…" It caused great pause for many that saw it on social media. What a great reminder for us today. We must be ready, or we WILL miss His return, or the opportunity for a life-saving relationship with Him.

Are you ready? If you are not, all you need to know is that God loves you. He loves you so much that He sent His son to give His life that your sin could be forgiven. The Bible says that we are all sinners, and the wages of sin is death, but that God sent His son to pay that price, for your sin and mine. All we need to do is ask Him to forgive us and welcome Him into our heart. If you can picture your sin written on a huge slate and Jesus wipes that slate clean, and stamps it "paid in full." It will never be held against us again. He promises to come into our heart and give us His Holy Spirit to help us live for Him for the rest of our lives. So if you have never asked Him to forgive you and asked Him into your heart, don't wait. Do it today. He's waiting for you, arms open to receive you.

The scripture tells us that when we ask Him into our heart, He comes in and has fellowship with us. Remember that old picture of Jesus standing at the door and knocking. Pull it up online and look at it. Just Google: "Jesus standing at the door knocking." You will find it. Notice that there is no doorknob on that door. You must open the door from the inside and welcome Him in. He loves you and is waiting for you to open the door.

Don't wait to share the truth of God's Word with others. God loves people so much that He made a way to have a relationship with them, today and in to eternity. God bless you friend. As the old timers used to say, "See you here, or there, or in the air."

Reflection

1. If you have never asked Jesus to forgive you and to come into your heart, do it now. Pray with me:

Dear God – I believe in You. I believe that You sent Your son to die for me. I hear You, I feel You knocking on my heart's door. Please come in like You said You would in Your Word. I know I am a sinner, lost without a relationship with You. I want a relationship with You. Please forgive me of all my sin. I ask You to wipe my slate clean and to stamp my debt "paid in full." Show me how to live for You the rest of my days. In Jesus name. Amen.

Please know that there are angels in heaven rejoicing right now because you just gave your heart to Jesus. Tell someone what you just did. Find a Bible believing Church and begin to read your Bible. Jesus said you are now His disciple. You must grow healthy in Him and that will happen through your relationship with Him and His people.

2. If you have struggled with sharing your faith, I encourage you to find a good class at a local church that will help you see how easy it is to simply tell others what Jesus did for you.

Make a list of people right now that you know don't know Christ. Begin to pray for them every day. The Bible says that nobody comes to God except that the Holy Spirit draws them. Just like He drew you, He will draw them. Ask God to use you to show them the great love, mercy and grace of the God that loves them and has a plan for their lives too.

PUT SOME "EXTRA" IN YOUR ORDINARY

We have seen God do incredible things in His people as they trusted Him for the impossible. I read yesterday morning in a devotion by Steven Furtick: "If you're not daring to believe God for the impossible... you're sleeping through some of the best parts of your Christian life. And further still, if the size of your vision for your life isn't intimidating to you, there's a good chance it's insulting to God."

Whoa! Insulting God? I'm thinking so. He's given us each a calling to be His hands, His feet, His voice, and be Jesus with skin to those in our sphere of influence. Life isn't random friends. God orders our days "on purpose." What's God's purpose for you today?

I preached a message not long ago about how God uses ordinary things to do extra-ordinary things. He allowed a stick to lift up an ax head in the water (come on, you know that's impossible). God met a need through someone who had compassion on another AND an ordinary stick. Read it in ***II Kings 6***. Amazing story of ordinary people doing what they were supposed to do, ran into a crisis, and God shows up through the one who was willing to do something. To the ordinary eye, it looked like a stupid thing to do. But to someone that trusts God to take those ordinary things, extra-ordinary things begin to happen.

Just like the woman with a little bit of oil. She had ordinary stuff, oil and a desire to not lose her sons into slavery. That's it! Listen to this:

II Kings 4:1-7 NIV *The wife of a man from the company of the prophets cried out to Elisha, "Your servant my husband is dead, and you know that he revered the Lord. But now his creditor is coming to take my two boys as his slaves."* [2] *Elisha replied to her, "How can I help you? Tell me, what do you have in your house?" "Your servant has nothing there at all," she said, "except a small jar of olive oil."* [3] *Elisha said, "Go around and ask all your neighbors for empty jars. Don't ask for just a few.* [4] *Then go inside and shut the door behind you and your sons. Pour oil into all the jars, and as each is filled, put it to one side."* [5] *She left him and shut the door behind her and her sons. They brought the jars to her and she kept pouring.* [6] *When all the jars were full, she said to her son, "Bring me another one." But he replied, "There is not a jar left." Then the oil stopped flowing.* [7] *She went and told the man of God, and he said, "Go, sell the oil and pay your debts. You and your sons can live on what is left."*

God takes what we give Him. What we give Him, He cleanses and purifies. What He cleanses and purifies, He uses. And what He uses, brings glory to Him.

What will you give Him today? How will YOU trust Him today? Remember, it's ordinary people doing ordinary stuff that God turns into extra-ordinary. ***Ordinary days + God = Extra-ordinary!*** He's awesome!!! What will you trust Him with? Will you trust Him enough to take that same kind of leap of faith? Not questioning the whys - just to be obedient with the ordinary things? He does extra-ordinary things when we do. To you my friends, have an extra-ordinary day!

Reflection

1. What do you think made the woman with the two sons do something so odd?
2. What questions might you have had before doing what you were told?
3. What do you think the sons might have felt rounding up all the jars?
4. What miracles do you or someone you love have need of?
5. What steps might you make to start trusting Him with that miracle?

For the next four devotions, I want to look at some things that I call "Faith Squashers." To be real, there are way more than four, but we will focus on just the following four: Fear, Comparison, Insecurities and Unforgiveness. So hang tight. It could be a bumpy ride.

FAITH SQUASHER NO.1- FEAR

No matter where we look, there is a lot said about faith. We have faith in people, or we don't. We have faith that when we get in our car, that it's going to run. We have faith that when we buy something and put it on our credit card, that we will have the money to pay for it at the end of the month. We have faith that if we do the right things, the results we expect will happen. The scriptures say much about faith. This is one out of ***Hebrews 11***.

Hebrews 11:1 NLT *"Faith is the confidence that what we hope for will actually happen; it gives us assurance about things we cannot see."*

Real faith is based on things we can't see. Not calculated risk. If I put the money in the bank, I trust it will be there when I go to get it. That's trust. I first had to put the money in there, and trust that the bank will keep it for me until I need it. It's an investment. It's calculated.

Trust and faith are related, but not the same. Faith is different. It's having confidence based on what I CANNOT see.

The **Dictionary** defines **faith** as confidence or trust in a person or thing. Belief that is not based on proof.

I don't have any proof – yet I believe that something is going to happen, or that something is true. That's faith.

There are many things that fall into the category of being a faith squasher. Today, we will talk about one of them: **fear.**

Fear keeps us from having confidence of what we hope for. Fear is believing a distorted view of God, circumstances and the promises in God's Word. Faith believes, even if we cannot see. Fear squashes faith. It distorts reality according to the Word of God.

Fear doesn't come from God. Power, love and a sound mind come from God, but not fear.

II Timothy 1:7 NKJV *"For God has not given us a spirit of fear, but of power and of love and of a sound mind."*

If you are struggling with faith, check your fear-factor. If you feel fear, that's not power. If you struggle with fear, that's not love. Fear will leave you feeling like you don't have a sound mind. It throws off your ability to hear from God and walk in the power and authority He has for you. Fear keeps us focused on ourselves. When I am focused on myself, I don't see God clearly.

I heard of a well-known evangelist who struggled all night in prayer, battling the enemy and his powers, only to find out that what he thought was the enemy, wasn't the enemy at all. It turned out to be the fear of something that wasn't even there.

There is an acronym for fear:
F – False
E – Evidence
A – Appearing
R – Real

Sometimes, it's fear of the unknown. In this minister's case, he had misinterpreted something he thought he saw. Sometimes, however, fear can be based on things that we do actually see. I see evidence of a tornado that is headed toward us. My faith overrides my fear and I know that God will protect my family, no matter how close it may come. Because I have confidence in my God to take care of my family and me, my faith overrides my fear. When my fear overrides my faith, that is when it is destructive and hurtful to me.

It was never God's will for us to live in fear. Fear will indeed squash our faith and our ability to live in power, love and the sound mind that He has for us.

So in choosing to squash fear today, we must each make a decision to believe truth. Faith is a choice to believe the truth. Faith isn't often a feeling, but rather, it is a choice! What will you choose today? A day walking in faith, or a day wrapped up in fear, of who knows what? His will for you is power, love and sound mind. No matter the circumstances you are living in, faith is bigger than any fear. Choose faith today!

Reflection

1. What are some of the things that cause fear to rise up in you?

2. Are they fears that are based on facts? Or are they the "monster under the bed" fears?

3. What does God's Word say about those fears?

4. How can you practically find power, love and sound mind in the midst of a fear attack?

5. What will you do today to live THIS day in the power, love and sound mind that God promises?

FAITH SQUASHER NO.2 - COMPARISON

Comparison is something we all do. If you think you don't, walk with me for just a few minutes to look at some of the things we compare in our lives. To some degree, we all fall victim to comparing ourselves with other people and things.

I remember one morning sitting at my piano. I was struggling to play a very simple worship song to Jesus during my devotion time. I don't play well, I know just enough to be dangerous. Don't feel sorry for me or wish you could encourage me that I would feel better. Really it's really OK, it is what it is. If I truly wanted to be better I'd take lessons or practice.

I only play for Jesus and me. That particular day I was lamenting, my heart really wishing I could play better for the love of my life, my God. "God, please help me," I prayed. "I listen to my friend David Kaap and I just wish I could play like David. If I could only worship You like David does on his piano." God responded to me loud and clear, in the depth of my soul: "Laurie – when you play for Me, I hear a symphony."

I realized at that moment that comparison really kept my eyes focused on my inadequacies and not on my ability to use what I had to worship Him. It kept me focused on me, not Him.

If we are honest, we would admit that we compare our stuff or ourselves more often than we think. We compare our families, our spouses, cars, houses, and even our ministries, whatever. If only I could be like that, then my life would be so much better.

Comparison keeps me focused on what I don't have, rather than being grateful for what I do have. We become selfish, envious, and never realize our full potential in Christ, all because we don't see ourselves as good enough.

We will never fully walk in faith if we live a life of comparison. We struggle to find that beautiful place of contentment that the Word tells us about because comparison is a cancer to contentment. Like cancer eats away at our body, comparison eats away at our contentment and destroys our faith.

> ***Comparison is a cancer to contentment.***

Robert Madu says: "Comparison will consistently cloud the clarity of God's call on your life."

We can't see God and His call when we consistently compare ourselves, our family, ministry or anything else.

II Corinthians 10:12 NIV *"We do not dare to classify or compare ourselves with some who commend themselves. When they measure themselves by themselves and compare themselves with themselves, they are not wise."*

We need to kill our comparisons – or our comparisons will kill our faith walk. Why? Because comparison is a three-headed monster: it leads to jealousy, selfishness and feelings that we will never quite measure up. It's more serious than we've ever realized.

Jealousy is truly resenting God's goodness in other people's lives and ignoring God's goodness in our own life. Listen to this:

James 3:14-16 NLT *"But if you are bitterly jealous and there is selfish ambition in your heart, don't cover up the truth with boasting and lying. For jealousy and selfishness are not God's kind of wisdom. Such things are earthly, unspiritual, and demonic. For wherever there is jealousy and selfish ambition, there you will find disorder and evil of every kind."*

Comparison has its roots in jealousy and selfishness. We must cut it off! There is only one antidote to comparison. To cut it off or to kill it means I have to suffocate it.

Craig Groeschel said in his book **#struggles:**
"Identify bad influences and celebrate others successes. Suffocate the flames of envy with a blanket of gratitude. Cultivate gratitude!"

The only way to squash comparison is to begin to cultivate an attitude of gratitude. God has created you to be YOU. In you are all the gifts and abilities He designed you to have. Celebrate the gifts He's given others and celebrate the gifts He's given you.

To walk in power and faith – celebrate God's goodness in others, and rejoice in all He has made you to be. If you haven't discovered your own gifts yet, talk to your Pastor or Ministry Leader. I'm guessing they can set you on a path to discover them.

Rejoice; Celebrate – squash any hint of comparison in your life.

Reflection

1. What areas of your life do you tend to compare with others?
2. How do you feel when you fall into comparing your life with someone else's life?
3. Learning that cultivating an attitude of gratitude is the antidote to comparing, what might you begin to thank God for in your own life?
4. What steps might you take to help you stay grateful for what God has made you to be?
5. In what ways can you celebrate God's goodness in the lives of those around you?

FAITH SQUASHER NO.3 - INSECURITIES

The last two days we have talked about fear and comparisons. Both of them will squash our faith in a heartbeat. Today, we will talk about the third one: **insecurities.**

Even seemingly strong and secure men and women have dealt with this at some level, at some point in their lives they have felt the pain of insecurity.

God has created each one of us with needs that will be met by someone or something. The REAL reason God gave us those needs is that He is the only one that can meet them. He desires to have an intimate relationship with each of us, and created within us a need for the same thing. We however, look to other things and people to get those needs met.

Looking to get those needs met in the wrong places can very well interfere with our faith. So, Faith Squasher No. 3 could be called "looking for love in all the wrong places."

If we're married, we think our spouse is to meet all our needs. If we're not married, we think other people or other things will meet those needs.

Most of us at some point in our life run hard and fast to have these needs filled, and still end up empty. It's like trying to get a drink of water out of an empty well.

The enemy tricks us by taking the things and people we enjoy and encourages us to look there for satisfaction. In the end, those people or things end up sucking the life out of us. And we continue to feel a loss and emptiness and don't know why.

God created every human being with four basic needs:

- **Acceptance.**
  We all want to know that we are accepted by someone. God is the one that gave us that need, because He wants to fill us completely with His grace, mercy and love. Then we are able to walk confidently every day knowing He accepts us and holds us securely in His hand. ***Psalm** 73:23*

- **Purpose.**
  God created each one of us with purpose and a desire to fulfill that purpose.

  Jeremiah 29:11-13 NIV *"For I know the plans I have for you," declares the Lord, "plans to prosper you and not to harm you, plans to give you hope and a future. Then you will call on me and come and pray to me, and I will listen to you. You will seek me and find me when you seek me with all your heart."*

  It's really clear, isn't it? Yet, what do we do? We look for our purpose in other things and people. We end up wandering aimlessly and continually wonder what our purpose is. I've heard so many people say, "What does God want from me?" Your heart dear one, it's your heart He wants. When He has your heart, you will seek Him and walk in your God-given purpose every day.

- **Security.**
  We are secure in Him. Nothing can tear us away from Him. We can choose to walk away, and that's precisely what we do when we look for security in people and things. We ARE secure in HIM. He loves us desperately. ***Romans 8:38***

- **Identity.**
  Jeremiah 1:5 NLT *"I knew you before I formed you in your mother's womb. Before you were born I set you apart and appointed you..."*

  Your identity is found in the fact that you are a child of God. And there's a whole Bible that gives you the details of what that all means. Read it – EVERY day. You will find the peace you long for and the security you need to walk as a son or daughter of the Most High God.

So, which one of these do you struggle most with: Acceptance, Purpose, Security or Identity?

When we continue to look for love in other people or things, it's called: **The Principle of Transference**. Any time we turn to anything or anyone to meet those needs, it puts a pressure on them that they can never satisfy. They will die trying, and you will continue to be empty. God is the only one that can fully meet those needs because He is the one that gave you those needs.

I know this is a long devotion, but I have one more short story to convey to you how desperately God loves you and longs for you to trust Him to fill every need in your life.

Our son and his wife gave birth to their first child, a beautiful daughter, named Carina Marie. Within minutes of her birth, they put that sweet baby girl on a warming table as they tended to Mom. Our precious, tiny granddaughter was crying so very hard with her eyes closed tight. Our son walked over to the table and spoke to her. He reassured her that she was going to be OK, that he was right there. When he told her that, when she heard his voice, her desperate crying stopped. She quieted, and stayed quiet as long as she could hear his voice.

He walked back over to his wife, and within a very short time, Carina started crying again, so very hard. Our son went back over to her and watched the most amazing thing happen. He assured her once again that he was right there. He went on to tell her that he loved her and that both him and her Momma loved her so very much. With tears in his eyes recounting that story, our son said that this time, when she heard him saying that he loved her, her tiny eyes opened wide and they gazed at each other for the first time. Hearing of his love, they were face to face with a love that would last a lifetime. She knew His voice. When she heard him say he loved her, it gave her what she needed to open her eyes for the very first time and look at him.

That is the confidence God desires for you dear one. That at the sound of His voice, your heart would still. At hearing that He loves you and all will be well, your anxiety settles. That only comes through knowing that everything you need is found in Him. That only comes through intimately trusting Him and looking for Him in everything, absolutely everything.

You are accepted by Him! You are secure in Him. You have purpose and identity in Him. Open your eyes! Like little Carina did, open your eyes. He is telling you today that He loves you. He waits to embrace you with a loving relationship with you. That you would have the ability to walk in faith, knowing He is all you need.

Reflection

1. Which of those four things, acceptance, security, purpose and identity, is the hardest for you to trust God for?

2. Why do you think you struggle with going to Him for it?

3. Who or what have you been running to, other than God, to get that need filled?

4. What steps do you need to take to begin to trust Him with that area of your life?

5. If you see clearly that someone you love is struggling with going to others or things for His love, how will you begin praying for them today? Specifically, how will you pray?

FAITH SQUASHER NO.4 - UNFORGIVENESS

For the last three devotions, we have talked about three things that squash our faith. The first one was ***Fear***. The second was ***Comparison***, the third ***Insecurities***, and this one is ***Unforgiveness***.

Now, please don't check out. Please don't close the book, shut down your computer, iPad or smart phone. This is a tough subject. Even my computer doesn't like it. Every time I type unforgiveness, it underlines it in red telling me there's something wrong with the word. Think not? Try it.

Even online dictionaries don't have a definition for unforgiveness. It says, "Do you mean 'forgive'?" You can find "unforgiv***ing***ness," but not "unforgiveness." There are times in our lives that we act like there isn't even a word like that – or like it's a "bad word" that doesn't show up in the dictionary. Like some of those words you learned in the back alley as a kid, and you were later taught were wrong by someone in authority, or one of your parents.

Even though the word unforgiveness doesn't show up in the dictionary, you can find countless authors that have written wonderful works on the subject. Some on how toxic it is, some giving you steps to overcome it, and still others to help you see what forgiveness IS and what it is NOT.

In our heart of hearts, we know unforgiveness has grave consequences, but we continue to nurse our wounds, find ways to justify not forgiving someone for the wrong that was done to us. Truth be known, it will squash your faith, and the consequences to you are severe.

Matthew 6:14-15 NLT *"If you forgive those who sin against you, your heavenly Father will forgive you. But if you refuse to forgive others, your Father will not forgive your sins.*

In ***Matthew 18***, Jesus talks about the man that was forgiven much yet refuses to forgive the debt that another man owed him. Jesus showed clearly the consequence of such actions. When we refuse to forgive someone, the consequences fall on us. It is us that get hurt.

I once heard the youth leader and great speaker Jeanne Mayo say, "Unforgiveness is like allowing a person to live rent-free in your mind."

It costs you everything, utilities, wear and tear on the property, noise, dollars to put into the rent or mortgage, but costs them nothing.

The phrase I use often is that ***"unforgiveness corrodes the container that carries it."***

> ***"Unforgiveness corrodes the container that carries it."***
> ***Laurie Ganiere***

The cost of unforgiveness is too great. Forgiveness is a choice. It's not saying what they did was OK or right. It's choosing to not hold their sin against them any longer.

Jesus never says sin is ok and doesn't ask us to either. But when we come to Him, He forgives us and His Word tells us He throws our sin as far as the east is from the west – and He remembers it no more. I believe He says that He throws it as far as the east is from the west because you can't measure that. You can measure north and south. If you are going north, you can only do that so long, and eventually you are going south. If you are going south, there will come a point that you will eventually be going north. But that will never happen if you are going east. There will never be a time that you have gone so far east that you begin going west. Impossible.

God never holds our sin against us, and will never bring it up again. He throws it as far as the east is from the west – and He remembers it no more. It does not mean He has a bad memory, rather it means He chooses to never bring it up again.

Choosing to forgive someone is a decision between you and God. Rarely is it necessary to tell someone you forgive them. That's a whole other devotion. When we choose to tell them, unsolicited, what we're really doing is trying to extract some acknowledgement from them that what they did was wrong. Trying to get some "payment," if you will, from them for what they did to you. That's not forgiveness, that's vindication. That's not throwing it as far as east is from the west...and remembering it no more.

People have asked me throughout the years, how do you do that? How do you walk that out? I made it my motto years ago that "I will never give them an opportunity to say I dumped on them." I will always respond with respect, grace and forgiveness. I will leave the rest with God. It frees me.

Now, please know that forgiveness and boundaries are two separate issues. Boundaries are necessary not to protect us from other people, but rather to protect us from the bad decisions or choices they have made. Their bad actions or words will no longer hurt me. I put up healthy boundaries to make sure that is true. If you have a problem with boundaries, take a look at a book by Cloud and Townsend called ***Boundaries.***

Forgiveness is a choice – so is walking in faith. But if you refuse to forgive, you will also not be forgiven. The cost is eternal. The cost is to your soul, not theirs. Secondly, your unforgiveness will indeed squash your faith. The two can't co-exist. Make that decision today to forgive. Move on in faith. Ask God to help you walk in forgiveness. He understands. He forgave you.

For a much more in-depth study on forgiveness, please pick up a copy of R.T. Kendall's book ***Total Forgiveness.*** You won't be sorry. That's a promise.

Reflection

1. What have been the hardest things for you to forgive someone of?

2. What is your greatest fear in forgiving that individual or group of people?

3. What if you knew that forgiveness was a choice, and that it was a progressive thing, sometimes forgiving many times? Would that make it easier for you? (Many deep wounds leave scars that will last for a long time. In choosing today to forgive, the feeling of unforgiveness may come up again in you. With some things, it's a choice that has to be made many times. It's no less forgiven if you have to ask again. Relax. Breathe. Eventually your emotions will catch up with what you believe to be true. God forgave you; He will help you to forgive them as well.)

4. Jesus paid our debt and stamped it paid in full. That's what you forgiving that person is. Stamping the debt paid in full. They will never owe you anything ever again. What will you need God to help you with regarding that whole concept?

5. Rarely is it necessary to tell someone that you forgive them. It's a decision between you and God. Who will you ask to pray with you about the deep wound that you have? Make sure you choose someone that will not nurse your wound, but one that believes in the power of forgiveness and will help you walk that journey too.

6. Make that decision today to walk in faith. Unforgiveness will no longer squash your faith.

LOSING PERSPECTIVE

How is it that we can get so caught up in something that we lose all perspective of reality or other things that need our attention? We've all been there. I know I sure have. Something happens, and it grabs all of our emotional energy, that we can miss everything else that's going on around us.

I was reading today, in II Samuel about the death of Absalom, David's son. It's way too long for me to go in to the whole story, but you might stop right now and read it. ***II Samuel 19!***

The whole story is so sad in so many ways. I can only imagine the great grief that David had after Absalom's death. He was so totally caught up in his grief that he forgot about everything around him. And who could blame him, right? Sometimes, in those deep emotional places, we need someone to help us find our balance again. Otherwise, we will forget all of the good things, as well as those people that have invested themselves into us and maybe the situation too. So just what am I talking about?

I think everyone needs a Joab in their lives. Someone that will speak bold truth to us to help us focus on the things we're missing. Joab went into David's room and spoke what seemed to be very harsh words to him, considering the man just lost his son; but words that were so necessary in the grand scheme of things. The stakes were high and Joab knew it. After all, David was the King and you just didn't approach the King at any time you felt like it. So he took a very big risk by going in to talk to him.

II Samuel 19:5-7 NIV *Joab went to King David and said: "Today you have humiliated all your men, who have just saved your life and the lives of your sons and daughters and the lives of your wives and concubines.* [6] *You love those who hate you and hate those who love you. You have made it clear today that the commanders and their men mean nothing to you. I see that you would be pleased if Absalom were alive today and all of us were dead.* [7] *Now go out and encourage your men. I swear by the Lord that if you don't go out, not a man will be left with you by nightfall. This will be worse for you than all the calamities that have come on you from your youth till now."*

Yikes. Talk about a scolding or a wake up call. How did David respond? He accepted this reproof, shook off his grief, pulled up his big boy britches and acted like a King once again. He got his focus back.

It's so easy to get in a deep, dark place when something bad happens. At those times, we need a Joab around to help us remember the things that are needful, even in the midst of the difficulties that have encased us. The problem is that we usually want to sit in our mess during times like this. And we feel we have the right to do so. And most others around us think we deserve to as well. It's times like these that it just takes too much energy to do anything else, so we just hunker in our little bunker and isolate.

What do we really need? A Joab. That person that is close enough to us that we have learned to trust them. That one individual that will be brutally honest, because they see how high the stakes really are for us to just sit in that dark place. They love us enough to high five us in the forehead if it will help us get back on track. They will help us to regain a proper perspective in the midst of it all.

Is there a Joab in your life; that person that you would trust and will listen to? It's perspective friends. God knows just how much we need Him, and He will use others in our lives that we trust to help us gain the proper perspective even when walking through some of the worst of valleys.

Don't push them away. Heed their words. You've trusted them in the past; you may very well need to trust them again.

Reflection

1. Why is it so easy to fall into a pit when we've gone through severe life circumstances?

2. What do we think we need when we're in that dark place?

3. What kind of person would Joab need to be that we would trust what he or she says?

4. How is it possible to refocus even during such deep loss?

5. What scriptures can you think of that give hope in time of deep, dark struggle?

6. Do you have a Joab in your life? If not, are you willing to invest in a relationship that would be that trusting?

REDEEM THE TIME

I had someone mention to me the other day that waiting for God's blessing is just so hard. They love God. They have a relationship with Him. They know that He is true to His Word. They believe that He will do what He promises. But...it's just so hard to wait.

Trials continue, things get worse and our faith starts to fade. Then we feel really guilty when our faith starts to sink. Then this crazy cycle of waiting begins; faith waning followed by guilt start a dance in our hearts and one thing feeds off the other in a downward spiral.

Stop the cycle! I just wanna get off. In order to do that, we need to shake off the guilt and re-think a few things.

A couple questions I would ask:

- Am I asking the right questions about the trial and waiting?
- Am I focusing on the awaited blessing so much that I am missing an opportunity?
- Is it possible that God may want me to redeem the time and find the treasure in it?
- Might there be a bigger reason in it all?

Acts 16 is a clear example of redeeming the time. Paul and Silas had confidence that this whole situation of being beaten, stripped and bound by chains had more to do with God's over all plan than it did their getting free. They were in an awful situation. What did they do? They redeemed the time and made it count for God.

Read it – ***Acts 16***. After being stripped, beaten and put in stocks, they were praying and singing hymns to God. How crazy is that? Seriously. I wonder how would I have reacted in their situation? Of course I can see praying. But singing hymns to God after being beaten and put in stocks in the deepest part of the dungeon? My prayer would only be for God to get me out of there. Send your angels, your people or something and just get me out.

But listen to this: Their focus was on the bigger picture, not just getting set free from the jail. How do I know that? Well, an earthquake came, blew the doors off the prison and their chains fell off, as did all the chains of the other prisoners, AND **they didn't run out the door**. They could have taken that as their sign and gotten out of the prison.

I don't know about you, but I'm thinking if it had been me, I'd have likely seen this as God answering my prayer, and I would have grabbed my Nikes and headed out the door.

But they realized that what was going on wasn't just to free them, but to accomplish a greater work to be done with them being in there. They chose to redeem the time. And because of it, others came to faith in their God.

Their eyes were not on THEIR blessing, but on BEING a blessing, a vessel that God works through.

> ***Their eyes were not on THEIR blessing, but on BEING a blessing.***

Imagine all the chaos after the earthquake. It was dark, all the stocks fell off and the prisoners freed. The jailer drew his sword and was ready to kill himself. Because it was dark, he thought surely all the prisoners had escaped. It was his job to guard them, and now he thought they had all escaped. He had failed miserably. What he didn't know was that it was all part of a greater plan.

Paul shouted to him, "Don't kill yourself. We're all here." It goes on to say the jailer accepted Christ. Then he took Paul and Silas to his home and it says his whole household was saved.

God's plans are so far beyond what we can think or imagine. God uses every situation and person. Our life is orchestrated to a much bigger plan than we can think or imagine. Nothing is random.

Corrie Ten Boom, great woman of faith, who spent much time in a concentration camp, said: ***"Every experience God gives us, every person He puts in our lives is the perfect preparation for the future that only He can see."***

Nothing in life is random. Will I choose to focus on the one who holds my life in His hands, and how He might use it in a way that will bring Him glory? Or will I only think about my own comfort? God will redeem everything in our life that we commit to him. Everything!

My prayer today is that you will choose to commit everything to Him, to be used by Him. Good, bad and ugly. Keep your eyes on Him. Focus on Him. Redeem the time – every day.

Reflection

1. What are the kinds of arguments you have with yourself during times of struggle?

2. In what ways have you seen God use something bad for something good?

3. What do you need to remind yourself of when those bad things arise?

4. How is it possible for God to use evil for good?

5. Who can you encourage to redeem their time during a trial?

6. How will you pray for them?

DO GOOD

Psalm 37:3-4 NIV *"Trust in the Lord and do good; dwell in the land and enjoy safe pasture. Take delight in the Lord, and he will give you the desires of your heart."*

This scripture brings back a flood of memories of our early days serving Christ. A friend back then, a great singer, songwriter, in the early 70's, Tom Dank, wrote a song about "Trust in the Lord and do good, good, good, good. Trust in the Lord and do good, good, good, good..." The melody rings in my head and heart even as I type this scripture.

Over the years we have seen the faithfulness of God, over and over and over again. As we trust Him and DO what is right, He promises that we will dwell in safe pastures. Also, as we "take delight in Him," He gives us the desires of our hearts.

I also have seen over the years, so many that just sit back and wait for God to do, give, fill, water, provide, heal, deliver, whatever. They don't sense any responsibility to DO anything. There can even be a weird kind of spiritual pride that declares, "I'm waiting on God," while I sit and do nothing. This scripture flies in the face of that theology.

It says, "Trust in the Lord and DO GOOD." It says, "TAKE DELIGHT" in the Lord. We must DO what is ours to DO.

Dr. David Jeremiah talks about this Divine Cooperative – that it's 100% God and 100% man. We DO what there is to DO and He partners with us to accomplish that which only He can do.

We had the privilege of attending a banquet with Dr. Ben Carson as the keynote speaker. If you've ever read Dr. Carson's book or seen the movie, ***Gifted Hands***, you know he overcame more obstacles in his life than many of us ever did or will. Through it all, he has learned the secret to living in safe pasture. He has learned the secret of receiving the desires of his heart.

He learned some hard lessons, from an early age. And today, even though he is now retired, he is a world-renowned neurosurgeon.

As Dr. Carson recounted his life for us, and all that he overcame, he gave a simple acronym for anyone who wants to unleash their potential excellence. It's THINK BIG.

T – Talents. God has given you talents. Every person – find out what they are
H – Hope and Honesty.
I – Insight – Learn from others.
N – Nice. Just be a nice person.
K – Knowledge - He said we can ALL have knowledge – we can ALL learn. He said "take it from a neurosurgeon your brain will never run out of room."

B – Books.
I – In-depth learning for knowledge and understanding.
G – GOD. The foundation of it all is your relationship with the God that has a plan for all men and women.

So, some lessons from the good doctor - THINK BIG!

Stop making excuses about the how's and why's and tap into your relationship with God and the plans He has for you. **Trust in the Lord and DO good**.

We have a responsibility that brings with it many blessings from the one we entrust all things to.

One of the last things you want to be when Jesus returns is just sitting on our "blessed assurance" and waiting. I'm not sure there will be a "well done faithful servant" following that. So just get started!!!! Unleash your potential for excellence. One thing at a time! Start! DO it!

Reflection

1. What is going on in your life right now that you have had trouble seeing God in?

2. Why is the "do" part so hard in that scripture? *"Trust in the Lord and do good."*

3. What area of your life have you longed for God to move? How have you neglected the "do" part?

4. What steps will you take today to "do good" as you wait and trust in the Lord?

A TIMELY WORD

Proverbs 15:23 NIV *"A person finds joy in giving an apt reply— and how good is a timely word!"*

How good is a timely word. God withholds none of them from us.

Every day, He knows just what we need, and gives it to us in the Bible, His Word. Those Words from Him are like a fresh drink of water that nourishes our soul. Or it certainly speaks to us about what we are going through or will face throughout the day. He also gives us opportunity to share that fresh word with others. There have been numerous times I have been in conversation with someone, and He will bring back just the right "timely word," that they may need to hear.

I recently had breakfast with a good friend. I haven't seen her in nearly a year, and we were reminiscing about a time in her life when she should have been on her death-bed. Today, doctors marvel that she is alive, and living life to its fullest. Very few survive long with the cancer that she had. In our recent discussion, I told her that I've lost count of how many people I have shared her story with. It is a story of the miracle healing following a surgery that should have just bought her some time. Instead, it was the beginning of a whole new life for her.

I remember that morning of her surgery so very well. I had gotten up way before sunrise to meet her at the hospital to pray with her before she was taken to the OR. I read my Bible before I left, book of ***John chapter 11, verse 4***, the story of Lazarus. Jesus said: *"This sickness is not unto death, but for the glory of God, that the Son of God may be glorified through it."* Then He said to me, "Tell Sue, this sickness is not unto death, but for the glory of God."

I began running scenarios through in my mind. "But Lord, this is the story of Lazarus. He DID die. I know you raised him from the dead, but golly Lord, just what are you saying? Are you gonna raise my friend from the dead?" And a bazillion questions to follow. God was patient with me. When I finished babbling, He said, "Just tell Sue this sickness is not unto death, but for My glory."

My fear was this, was I hearing from God or is this what I wanted to believe? I loved my friend, and couldn't bear the thought of losing her. I think if you are honest, you'd wonder the same thing.

That was a great number of years ago. Sue is very much alive and astounding doctors still today when they look at her history and remind her that people don't recover from that cancer.

That "timely word" encouraged me, to be sure, but it also encouraged her right before she underwent surgery. That "timely word" built faith in me as I trusted Him to take that word and breathe life into my friend and indeed use it to bring glory to Him.

The main reason for this devotion is to tell you to get into His Word every day. Word is breath, health, life, encouragement, love, grace and mercy. Yes it is a love letter to us. But it is the track for us to run on every day, and an opportunity for us to share that word with those in our sphere of influence, not that they would think we're all that smart or cool. But rather, *"for the glory of God, that the Son of God may be glorified through it."*

Read His Word - Share a timely word.

Reflection

1. Recall a time when God brought back to you a "timely word."

2. How did He use you with that word?

3. How do you second-guess yourself when sharing a word with someone?

4. What can you do next time to help you step out in faith, trusting that word for a friend?

THE END IS IN SIGHT

"The End" is usually what we see at the conclusion of a book, a short story, in the last seconds of a movie, or often on social media after someone has made a simple statement, followed up with "the end." We expect there to be nothing following "the end." After all, it IS "the end."

I remember, a number of years ago, we were going through a very difficult season at the church we were attending. I was on the administrative staff and there were daily struggles that were very emotionally exhausting. One of those days, on the way to the office, I was praying and asking God for an extra measure of grace for the day. I arrived at the office, walked up to my desk, and saw a gift that some anonymous person had left for me. It was the **Precious Moments** figure shown in the picture. The caption on the figurine is, ***"The End is in Sight."***

I felt an immediate extra measure of grace to begin my day. I know God has a great sense of humor. He knew exactly what I needed and when I needed it. To this day, I have no idea who put it there. So it really is a gift of grace from my God.

Today, no matter what you may be going through, know that God is the grace giver. His mercies are new every morning. We don't always feel them, but we step out in faith believing that it is true. Sometimes we get a little gift from Him showing us His grace and mercy. Sometimes it's a word or a hug from a friend. Sometimes it's encouragement right from His Word, aimed at your heart like an arrow. Other times, it's just a feeling, that as good as your knower can know, you know He's not forgotten you and will give you all you need for the day. Yet another day, it may be that unexpected gift, from Him, given by an angel that you will never see.

James 5:7-11 NIV *"Be patient, then, brothers and sisters, until the Lord's coming. See how the farmer waits for the land to yield its valuable crop, patiently waiting for the autumn and spring rains.* [8] *You too, be patient and stand firm, because the Lord's coming is near.* [9] *Don't grumble against one another, brothers and sisters, or you will be judged. The Judge is standing at the door!* [10] *Brothers and sisters, as an example of patience in the face of suffering, take the prophets who spoke in the name of the Lord.* [11] *As you know, we count as blessed those who have persevered. You have heard of Job's perseverance and have seen what the Lord finally brought about. The Lord is full of compassion and mercy."*

Look at the **Precious Moments** figurine on my desk. The puppy pulling at the little guys jeans, showing his behind. All the while he's reading his Bible. The end is in sight friend. Until then, His mercies are new every morning and His grace is sufficient. Be patient. Blessed are those who have persevered.

God be with you! The end is in sight!

Reflection

1. Knowing that seasons can last a long time, what do you need most when you are in the midst of a difficult one?

2. What emotion do you battle most with when a season lasts so long?

3. Where do you tend to go for strength and encouragement?

4. What does God give you to help you persevere?

5. Who do you know right now that is going through a difficult season that may need an encouragement from you?

COMPANY LOYALTIES AND LABELS

Company loyalties, we all have them: favorite brands of food, restaurants, cars, motorcycles, clothing, jewelry, hunting gear, bug spray, even essential oils. My favorite motorcycle is Harley Davidson (HD). I've been riding my own for some time now, and can't imagine myself on any other kind of motorcycle. And that also includes their motor clothing line. Harley riders do a lot of things that many don't understand.

We go to every bike rally we can within riding distance. And truly, there isn't much that isn't within riding distance unless there's an ocean between.

We go to events and HD dealers to ogle all the bikes there, not necessarily wanting a new one, but admiring those bikes that are an expression of another owner's love for their HD. Cuz it's a company loyalty.

When we are out on the road, we will "salute" as we pass a Harley plant or dealership. We're loyal to Harley riders too. You will see bikers give a hand signal passing on the road. It's not that they're trying to be cool, they truly care about each other. Personally, I pray for them as I pass them.

As a female rider, I have a shirt that says: “Whoever said diamonds are a girls best friend has never owned a motorcycle.” Bikers often even name their bike: mine is “Clairee” from the movie ***Steel Magnolias***. She’s classy and sassy.

One main thing about company loyalties or labels is that if it’s not your thing, you don’t understand all the stuff that goes with it. Many think it’s really foolish. I would submit that it’s the same with being a Christian. People that do not know Jesus, really think Christian is just another label and isn’t one for them.

They don’t understand how crazy Christians are overcome with emotion at times with the thought that Jesus is REAL, and involved in their lives in every way. Every breath, every action, every thought is consumed or directed by that relationship with Him. That when you come into relationship with Jesus, your life turns upside down, or should I say right side up?

Many people think that being a Christian is all about what “label” church you go to. Though church is very important, it’s a relationship with the real God that makes us a Christ Follower, or Christian. People say, well, I’m Catholic; or I’m Lutheran; or I’m Baptist; or I go to a Community Church, or I’m____________, you fill in the blank. That dear friends, is a label. My church can’t save me. My church can’t change me. Only a relationship with Jesus can do that.

In the Gospels, ***Matthew, Mark, Luke*** and ***John***, there is much said about a group of people that were called Pharisees. They firmly believed that everything that made us good or right with God was to DO the right things. They really believed that to get to heaven, you had to obey the rules. That is only partially true.

Today Pharisees would say things like: "You're going to the wrong "label" church"; "You can't wear those kinds of clothes to church." They might say, "You can't eat this or drink that." Modern day Pharisees truly believe that it's all about doing the right things, not becoming the right thing. They tried to do that to Jesus and his followers too. Even Jesus was criticized for not following the laws of their label.

Jesus really messed up their rules. Jesus is still messing up rules in people's lives. See here's the thing: people that thought they had their stuff together (Pharisees) didn't see their need for grace, mercy and love. They lived their lives to follow the rules and work their butts off to get to heaven.

But when Jesus came, He showed them that they could never make themselves good enough for God. And that really messed up their heads. He sacrificially gave His life to pay the penalty for our sin, so that you and I could have a relationship with Him. Accepting that, believing that, opening our heart to Him is how we enter into a relationship with that God. Not through our works. Our works result from our relationship with Him, but they don't gain us entrance into heaven.

Jesus taught that love, mercy and grace ranked above the rules. He knew the message the Pharisees taught stole truth and prevented people from a real relationship with Him.

Jesus said in ***John 10:10 The MSG*** *"A thief is only there to steal and kill and destroy. I came so they can have real and eternal life, more and better life than they ever dreamed of."*

He came to give us life. When we accept Him as Lord and Savior, His Holy Spirit comes to live inside us, to give us life, real joy, real peace, real grace, love and mercy. He loves us. He's so much more than a lousy label. He's REAL.

Until you experience Him, you will not truly understand. Until you know as good as your knower can know, that Jesus loves you and wants a REAL relationship with you, you will dismiss Him as a label or a preference, like a choice between a Harley and a Honda or Suzuki.

If you have not found that relationship with Him, I encourage you to simply ask Him. Prayer is just a conversation with you and Him. Ask Him to come in to your heart. Ask Him to forgive you and help you to live the life He created you to live. He loves you. He's waiting for you with open arms.

Don't worry about a label. Just focus on a new relationship with Him. Get yourself into a good Bible believing church that preaches a Gospel like you just heard. Jesus is the way, the truth and the life. No one comes to the Father, but through Him. It's not a label. It's a relationship.

If we can help in any way, please email us at resourcemin@gmail.com and we will pray with and for you.

Reflection

1. What kind of labels or company loyalties do you have?

2. How deep are those loyalties?

3. What's the difference between a label and relationship when it comes to your spiritual life?

4. What areas do you need help to get your eyes off your labels and on to Jesus?

5. What will you pray today to help you draw closer to Jesus, "the way, the truth and the life"?

CHEAP CANDY

Scenario:
You're sitting down sharing a cool beverage on a hot day. You're enjoying catching up and having some laughs along with some serious conversation with a good friend. At some point, your friend tells you something about a mutual friend. It's not a good thing, like how proud they were of said friend or how much they love them. Rather it's something bad about your mutual friend. Possibly something that someone said about your mutual friend that would hurt them deeply if they knew that someone was talking about them. In other words, gossip.

So, what do you do? Do you stop the conversation before it gets juicy? Telling your friend that you really don't want to get into gossip about a mutual friend? Or do you lap up the information like a parched puppy on this 95 degree day? Most often we, as human beings, lap it up and then feel guilty about it later, or pass it on to someone else to "clarify" the validity of it, or worse yet, tell the person that was talked about that things are being said.

Whew – that was a longer scenario than I intended. But here's the thing. Over the years I've seen this happen over and over and over again. People hurt by what others are saying. I have often made the statement "why in heaven's name did you feel it was appropriate to tell me about this?" Or "why in the world did you think it was the right thing to tell them something like that, knowing it would hurt them desperately?"

The scriptures call it gossip. Justify it however you want. It's gossip.

Once you tell that friend what was said, they feel AWFUL that others are talking about them, or feel totally offended that someone would actually feel that way about them. It hurts them and does nothing to protect them or build them up.

As Christ followers, we should always look to the Word to determine if something needs to be spoken. There are a lot of people that say, "well I'm telling the truth," like truth telling means you tell the whole world bad things you've heard. There's no honor in that.

Scripture says in ***Proverbs 16:23-24 NLT*** *"From a wise mind comes wise speech; the words of the wise are persuasive. Kind words are like honey— sweet to the soul and healthy for the body..."*

Kind words are like honey. They are sweet. Not hurtful and destructive.

Proverbs 16:27-28 NLT *"Scoundrels create trouble; their words are a destructive blaze. A troublemaker plants seeds of strife; gossip separates the best of friends."*

Repeating such things are hurtful and create a destructive blaze. Troublemakers plant seeds of strife. Gossip separates the best of friends. How is it we can think that it's "helpful" to tell them what someone has said about them??? That's twisted.

How is it that we can think it's ok to even listen to words that tear down someone else?

Proverbs 18:8 MSG *"Listening to gossip is like eating cheap candy; do you really want junk like that in your belly?"*

Cheap candy tastes good – but it's terrible for your gut. Gossip is the same way. The affects of ingesting something toxic can be deadly to our soul.

Then to think that we should pass that toxic mess on to someone else? That's why the Word talks so much about the dangers of gossip.

Over the years, I've seen so many people hurt by others when things were passed on that should have never been spoken. If we are honest, I believe we can all admit to the fact that we've gotten trapped in the same kind of scenario. Either the one repeating something we heard, or we were the recipients of something that was said about us. Either way, it was gossip and toxic to our souls.

We need to take heed of the Word that says: *"Kind words are like honey— sweet to the soul and healthy for the body."*

Prayer:

God forgive me for causing hurt with my words. Help me to forgive those that have passed on toxic words that caused deep wounds in me. Let Your healing ointment cover me and heal those hurts. God help my words be kind today, sweet to my soul and kind and uplifting to those that I talk to. In Jesus name. Amen.

Reflection

1. Explain how you felt while reading this.

2. Why is it so easy to get trapped into gossip conversations?

3. What kind of healthy boundaries can you set for yourself for when you speak with others?

4. What will you do next time someone says something to you about another brother or sister?

5. If there is some conversation that you know you should never have been a part of, take it to God right now, and ask Him to forgive you.

6. I would encourage you to ask God if it would be beneficial to go to the ones you hurt with your words and ask their forgiveness. It's hard to do, but He will help you. Ask Him. He will confirm it to you.

HE'S PRAYING TO ME RIGHT NOW

Acts 9:10-12 NLT *"Now there was a believer in Damascus named Ananias. The Lord spoke to him in a vision, calling, "Ananias!" "Yes, Lord!" he replied.* [11] *The Lord said, "Go over to Straight Street, to the house of Judas. When you get there, ask for a man from Tarsus named Saul.* **He is praying to me right now.** [12] *I have shown him a vision of a man named Ananias coming in and laying hands on him so he can see again."*

As I was reading this morning, there was this one sentence that jumped off the page. You know the kind. The ones that make you feel like you've never seen them before. It's the kind that has you wondering just when it was that He put THAT sentence in there. Surely it wasn't there before. I assure you – it's been there all the time. Today is when you REALLY needed to see it, so He illuminated it for you. That sentence for me this morning was: *"He is praying to me right now."* It's the story of Saul's conversion and how God spoke to Ananias in a vision to go to Saul and pray for him. As you can see, right in the middle of it, God says *"He is praying to me right now."*

I saw this enormous picture in my mind of a man on one side, praying, and on the other side, God is at the same time putting together the answer to His prayer by connecting the dots to make it so.

I don't know if that makes you shiver, but it sure does me. Even as we are uttering the words in prayer, He is already working. We may not see the evidence of it right away. After all, it took some time for Ananias to do what God directed him to do. There's a lot we don't know.

If you are the "pray-er" today, you can rest assured that as you pray, God is already connecting the dots in answer to your prayer.

We live in such a fast paced society, that if we don't get a response right away, it is hard to continue to trust that God is really in control. Or there are trials so deep and wide that we are sure that He has forgotten us. Please dear ones, reject that lie from the enemy of your soul. Your God has not forgotten you, never will, not gonna happen! While you pray, He IS working. His timing is perfect. He knows the desperation of your cry. He knows the real need inside the need. He wants even more than you for your crisis or need to point people to Him.

> ***As people see us face crisis, they see real people with real problems that trust a real God.***

As Christians, we want our lives to glorify Him. What that means in a simple sense is that my life and everything in it would point to Him. As people see us walk through difficulties, we continue to trust Him. ***As people see us face crisis, they see real people with real problems that trust a real God.*** The God that is so great that even as we are praying

He is working out an answer or series of events that will all point to His goodness, love, grace and mercy. What is in your life today that you need to trust Him for? What are you praying about that you need to have that picture of Him already orchestrating your rescue? Know that He is greater. ***Know that at the end of the day, your life, through your crisis or difficulty, can point real people with real problems to trust a real God.***

Reflection

1. When have you looked at someone in struggle and seen clearly that God was working?

2. How did you know it was God?

3. What did they do that helped you to see Him?

4. What is going on in your life, or the life of someone that you love, that you desperately want others to see you as real?

5. Many times people fear that if they're "too real," that it will show others more than they want them to see. Define real people and real problems in your own words.

6. What can you do moving forward to be more real so that others will see and trust their God that is real and willing to be working on their behalf?

IT'S A TRAP

We recently watched the movie, ***War Room*** again. It was released in 2015, but I am continually challenged to pray with greater focus after watching that movie. How easy it is to fall into wimpy prayer traps. Maybe you are WAY more focused on praying specific in your prayer than others. But then, maybe it's easier for you to pray more generalized prayer. You know, those kind that are really simple like: "God bless them!" Of course we want God to bless them, but with what? For what, in what area of their lives do they need a touch from God? What's going on in their lives? Am I close enough to God that I sense His Spirit directing me to specific areas of prayer for my kids, their spouses, and my grandkids, family, neighbors and friends?

As I began working through the ***War Room Bible Study***, it asked a series of questions to honestly evaluate my prayer life. I began to see some very interesting patterns in myself. One of them relates to complacency and contentment. How easily I can confuse the two. I felt stunned when God pointed it out to me.

As a parent there are some times when all is well in the lives of your children. I mean, when I look at my kids, they're all working, paying their bills, they are reasonably healthy, spending quality time with their own families, investing in things that are valuable according to the Word of God. There is no greater feeling as their mother and "nana," than knowing all is well. There's a peace that comes over me, and I have always called it contentment.

Here's the thing God showed me that day, "Laurie it's not contentment, it's a trap for complacency." I said, "WHAT? Wait God. How can it be a bad thing to be content? You said in ***Philippians 4*** that the Apostle learned to be content in whatever state he was in. So now you're telling me not to be content?" He went on to say, "being content with the things you have and the state you are in is one thing. But that feeling of contentment with the lives of your kids and grandkids has led you to complacency in your prayer. You don't pray specifics for them, but generalities, when things appear to be going well." WOW! Just WOW! So, it's a trap. What I thought I was feeling was contentment and it was really a trap to keep my prayers wimpy as it relates to those I love most deeply this side of heaven.

Complacency can well be prayers of duty. It's my duty to pray for them, a duty I take seriously, so I pray, "God, bless them today."

Now if I'm serious about wanting God to intervene in their lives and truly reveal Himself to them today, it will change how I pray for them. I will pray specifics and ask the Holy Spirit to show me how to pray for them.

Just a little zig-zag. I'm thinking about all the "praying" that goes on in social media. How quickly we type "praying," "will pray for you," to a prayer request on social media. I'm just as guilty. It's like the Christian response to a prayer request. We want them to feel like we care, so we say, "praying." Most often, we really do pray. But how often do we forget as we scroll along the timelines? A long time ago, God reminded me that if I am going to tell someone I'm praying, I'd better pray. So if I write "praying," or "will pray for you," I do it right then. Otherwise we all know that if we don't, we will go on scrolling through timelines reading all kinds of stupid stuff and see pictures of what people ate for lunch and which beach they're at with their family and forget all about it until we see something again the next day or two. THEN we remember that we said we'd pray. So, do it right away. Don't wait.

I don't know if you see yourself in the same trap as I did; thinking I was content and really I had become complacent. If you have, please have a conversation with your Father about it today. Ask His forgiveness for complacency, and begin praying some serious prayer, pointed and specific for your family. There's a war to be won. Their souls and very lives are hanging in the balance. Seriously. Their souls are hanging in the balance.

God be with you!

Reflection

1. Have you ever felt completely content with the way your life was going? Explain why.

2. What needs, either in you or those you love, do you see need a touch from God?

3. Make a list of the details involved in those lives and prayer list for each.

4. Set a time that you will do some serious "war room" prayer for them and for you.

5. Right next to my "God Spot," is a wall hanging that says, "In the morning when I rise, give me Jesus." Family member Danny Gokey recorded that song on his Christmas Album "Christmas is Here."
   Pull it up on YouTube at: goo.gl/1MiwkP
   Listen right before your devotion time. I promise, it will change your devotion time and how you pray for those you love.

6. That our loved ones and family members, our neighbors, co-workers, everyone that is in our sphere of influence benefits from our prayer for them. That they feel the hand of God, His very thumb print on them. That they come to Him. That they would all one day say, "Just give me Jesus."

SPOILED OR BLESSED

I think we've all been privy to the behavior of what we would call a "spoiled child." That kid that gets everything he or she wants, and how they scream and throw a fit if they don't. Eventually the parent either exhausted from the fight, feeling out of their ability to deal, or just plain old lazy gives in to the little charmers desires. Over time that child learns how to get whatever they want and are willing to do whatever it takes for that to be so. That child never learns to be content, thankful, grateful or loving, only self-centered. They never learn true love and only learn to manipulate people to get what they want. I pray I'm never that spoiled kid.

I experienced a great number of blessings over the last several months with a health issue I have. With these repeated blessings, I began feeling like a spoiled kid. I mean really!!! I could go on and on about all the parking spaces that mysteriously opened up – like door-to-door spots. I have pulled in to a number of packed out parking lots and have spots by the door open up just when I approach. My health issue involves some breathing issues that make walking too far difficult. So this has been a BIG deal.

Like I said, I've begun to feel like a spoiled kid. I don't ever want to learn to "expect" it. One day while out on my motorcycle, I was talking to God just as I do a lot while riding. It was an especially beautiful day and I was thanking Him for the beauty and how grateful I am for all He allows me to do and to have such the rich life that I do. He spoke in that moment, tenderly, ever so sweetly, three simple words that were like gold to me, "I love you." It was so precious and unexpected that I began to tear up. That's not a good thing while riding a motorcycle, tearing up, I mean. I quickly thought, "This isn't a good time for this." I began to chuckle, helping to stop the tears. I'm pretty sure He was chuckling too.

Please know this: My relationship with my Heavenly Father is one of love, thankfulness and deep gratitude for all He is to me. If He gave me nothing from this day forward, He would owe me nothing. He is a wonderful, loving Father whose blessing is because of His goodness, not mine. My prayer is that this is the case for you as well.

Our relationship with Him and our attitude toward Him makes the difference between a spoiled kid and a blessed child. I don't expect good things, but enjoy them when I have them; but not nearly as much as He is blessed to give them to me. Let me explain.

To clarify what I just said, what my son Ricky recently posted on social media will help:

"I can't honestly say working weekends is on the top of my list but one of my favorite things happens on these weekend mornings. There is nothing quite like being the only car riding across the Hoan (Bridge) and catching a colorful sunrise over Lake Michigan. No traffic, no rush. It feels like for a second it's

just you and the universe. I'd say embracing it is a beautiful thing but ***it actually feels like the earth is embracing me and taking pleasure in my enjoyment of it.*** *Enjoy your weekend, friends."*

That's it!!! That's really it. God takes great pleasure in our enjoyment of all He does for us. Enjoy it. Be blessed to the depth of your soul because of it.

If you are a spoiled kid, you demand Him to "give me, buy me, bring me, take me." If you understand His great love and pleasure He takes in giving you what you NEED, not necessarily what you want, you can live with deep gratitude. That gratitude spills out to everyone in your sphere of influence. Let it be seen in you today.

Psalm 117:2 NIV "For great is his love toward us, and the faithfulness of the Lord endures forever. Praise the Lord."

Reflection

1. When was the last time you remember that God surprised you with a special blessing? What was it?

2. How does it make you feel knowing that God takes great pleasure in blessing you?

3. Explain a time when you may have felt you deserved a blessing and didn't feel you got one?

4. If you have been a spoiled child, what do you need to say to your Father today?

5. If you've been a blessed child, how can you convey to Him your gratefulness?

6. Who will you pray for today to find that sweet spot of receiving an unexpected blessing today?

WHO'S HOLDING WHO?

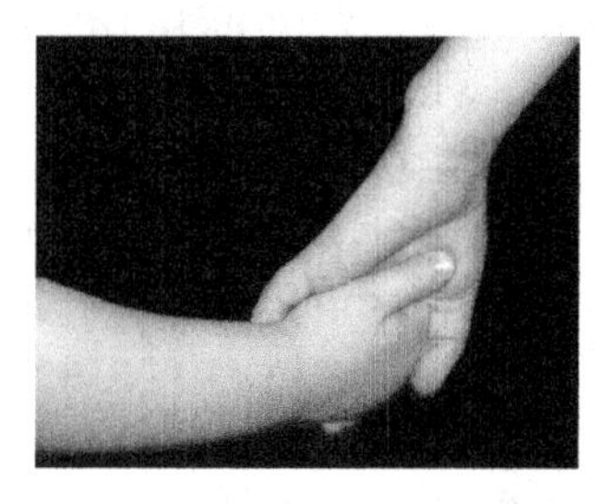

Recently I was out on a walk with our youngest grandchild, Carina. She is a precious little one, who loves nothing more than to be outside, no matter the weather. That particular day, it was HOT. She didn't care, but this Nana was melting in the heat and humidity. So I did what really came easy, even in the heat, and focused on her great joys in life. She is 20 months old, and loves picking up rocks, sticks, pinecones, smelling the neighbor's flowers (not picking them), and messing up ant hills. She will giggle with delight at finding just the right thing to add to her collection. She will be that kid one day that Mom will have to check her pockets before throwing laundry in the machine. Surely those little pockets will be filled with all kinds of treasures. Possibly even a bug or two.

As Carina and I were walking, she made it clear that she did not want to go home. So we prepared to cross the street in their quaint, little, quiet neighborhood. I reminded her that we could not cross the street without her holding Nana's hand. She willingly gave me her little hand and across the street we went.

I was quickly reminded of this scenario many times before. I recall walking across the street many moons ago with one of my kids and there was a car that approached, going way too fast for our family neighborhood. I squeezed that child's hand so tight that there was no way he was busting loose from my grip. God spoke to me clearly that day and said, "It's me that holds your hand, not the other way around."

It's so easy for us to think that we hang on to God for dear life when going through dangerous waters in our lives. We really think that if we just hang on, we'll make it through ok. When the truth is really that it's Him that's hanging on to us, not us hanging on to Him. If it were me hanging on to Him, my strength would never be enough to weather some of the great storms we've gone through. That's precisely why He shows us in His Word that He is the one doing the holding. It's dependent on Him, not us.

The psalmist wrote of God's care:
Psalm 63:8 NLT *"I cling to you; your strong right hand holds me securely."*

Psalm 66:9 NLT *"Our lives are in his hands, and he keeps our feet from stumbling."*

God was speaking about David when He said in
Psalm 89:21-22 NLT *"I will steady him with my hand; with my powerful arm I will make him strong. His enemies will not defeat him, nor will the wicked overpower him."*

It's His hands holding, steadying and protecting. It's Him that holds on to our hands, squeezing the sap out of them at times because we are like little kids and try to walk our own way. As my small son didn't see the danger with that approaching vehicle, I did. I squeezed on to him, so tight that there was no way he would be harmed on my watch. It was the same way that day with Carina. She's not even two yet, so she didn't rationalize this whole thing out. She didn't think, huh, cool, Nana's got me. No, she just walked confidently across the street, and I had her hand securely in mine. Do we have that same confidence in our God who's got our hand?

No matter what's going on in your journey right now, know that He's got your hand. Rest in His care. He's got this. You don't have to work hard to hang on. He's got you. Our family learned a number of years ago that no matter the crisis, God's got it. We learned that principle through the eyes of a very sick 11 year old who confidently said, "God's got it." He's got your hand. He steadies, protects, keeps you from stumbling and He will make you strong and keep you safe.

Reflection

1. When was the last time you remember being afraid because you weren't sure you could hang on to God through a storm?

2. What did you do to overcome the fear?

3. What word picture will help you to remember who's holding whom?

4. What can you share with another that is struggling to find comfort in the fact that "God's got it?"

TRUST IN THE LORD

The Word of God, the Bible, is truly dear to me. Though I love it all, there are, however, just some verses that get captured deep down in my soul for a lifetime. They come back over and over, through my life, as I've learned to trust Him in some of the most unusual situations. One of those scriptures for me is:

Proverbs 3:5-6 NLT "Trust in the Lord with all your heart; do not depend on your own understanding. Seek his will in all you do, and he will show you which path to take."

Trust Him. Don't depend on your own understanding. It doesn't have to make a lick of sense to me, and many times it does not. But I still trust Him. I've often said, "When we don't know what to do, we do what we know to do." We go back to His Word, we seek Him and He will show us which path to take. Most likely, one step at a time.

I was talking to a good friend recently who God was showing that it was time to take a step. Have you ever been there? You felt God pointing, telling, showing, some form of communication, even if it's just as good as your knower can know, that it's time to take a step. That sounds fairly simple. One step. In fact, it can sound really exciting if you enjoy change. But for the person who doesn't like change, it can be downright terrifying, and the thought of taking a step with no guarantees can literally take your breath away.

Even as I personally enjoy change, I like to know where we're going. Right? That's just basic. Don't you? Unless I'm on my motorcycle! I love the adventure and I truly don't care much where we're going. I follow the leader. The leader when we're riding is my husband. He's a wonderful leader and finds the most amazing roads. I've learned not to ask too many questions, but simply enjoy the journey and follow my leader. It's amazingly beautiful when I can trust him.

It's like that with God too. He wants that kind of trust from us as well. He knows the roads, He's got a path and will share it with us when we need to know. Sometimes God asks us to take an Abraham journey. ***Hebrews 11:8 NLT*** *"It was by faith that Abraham obeyed when God called him to leave home and go to another land that God would give him as his inheritance.* ***He went without knowing where he was going."***

When God tells us to do something, we don't have to know the "what" and "where" about it. We simply obey, in faith believing Him. Someone once said that when God asks us to take one step, rarely does he show us the whole staircase. We see one step at a time. We trust, one step at a time.

This little **Precious Moments** skydiver sits on my bookcase. He reminds me to simply ***"Trust in the Lord to the Finish."*** He has little wings on his back, goggles on his head and a helmet to protect him as he stands on a cloud looking down, a bit contemplative. He's carrying a little book under his arm that says, "Flying Lessons."

As we do what ***Proverbs 3:5-6*** tells us, we don't have to understand. Just seek Him. Trust Him. And He will show us the path. He's given us a manual of "flying lessons" in His Word, the Bible. So we seek Him and trust what we've learned.

My life has been filled with Abraham moments. God has called me from one place to another, with God simply saying, "It's time daughter. Follow me." When I get nervous and ask for clarification, He often says, "You will know when we get there. So, just trust me." I've learned to trust in some of the most unusual situations. There's no better scary-exciting place to be. Trust Him with all your heart. Don't lean on YOUR understanding. Seek Him in all you do, and He will direct you in the next steps.

God be with you friends. Trust Him.

Reflection

1. How have you felt during a time of uncertainty, a time that you really didn't know what was to come?

2. What do you do to help yourself simply follow and trust Him?

3. If you are in that place now, who will you get "real" with and share your concern? Godly friends can be key in helping us get back on track to trust Him. Who is that friend for you?

4. What practical advice would you give to someone else that would help them "trust in the Lord" and not lean on their own understanding?

A TIME FOR EVERY SEASON

This is a scripture that is familiar to most everyone:

Ecclesiastes 3:1-8 NIV
"There is a time for everything,
and a season for every activity under the heavens:
2 *a time to be born and a time to die,*
a time to plant and a time to uproot,
3 *a time to kill and a time to heal,*
a time to tear down and a time to build,
4 *a time to weep and a time to laugh,*
a time to mourn and a time to dance,
5 *a time to scatter stones and a time to gather them,*
a time to embrace and a time to refrain from embracing,
6 *a time to search and a time to give up,*
a time to keep and a time to throw away,
7 *a time to tear and a time to mend,*
a time to be silent and a time to speak,
8 *a time to love and a time to hate,*
a time for war and a time for peace."

Every time I read this scripture, there's a song that I hear in my head. If you are my age, you remember the song done by The Byrd's, "Turn, Turn, Turn." You can hear it in your head now, right?

I was reminded of this scripture yesterday as I was sharing with a friend about how God does all things in time. How He takes bad and uses it somehow for good, in us and through us. That we must understand that no matter where we are, God is at work. There is a time for everything. There is a season.

Our problem with the time factor is that we are very impatient people. If the trees in their budding were impatient, there would not be beautiful flowers or leaves. It takes time to develop, the seasons stretching over a sometimes long period of time.

Some years ago, Rick and I had a bad motorcycle accident. We both ended up being transported to the hospital, thankfully, with nothing broken, just a lot of stuff that took time for healing. I had a massive amount of what they called "road rash." I told the nurse, "This is no rash. I know rash, and this isn't it." What I had was NO SKIN down my arm and right leg. And it seemingly took forever, days that seemed like months to get all the asphalt out. The cleaning and healing was painfully slow.

Then there was infection that impeded the healing process. Finally, the doc called in a very wise dermatologist to look and give his opinion about how to proceed. What this man saw stunned me. He saw buds of healing when all I saw was raw, open, red flesh. He bent over and said, "Look. See that tiny white spot? That's new skin forming." I gotta tell you, I really had to strain to see what he saw. To me it looked smaller than a pin head. But he was right. There was a tiny spot. For the first time in a long time, I had hoped that healing just might come.

He gave me detailed instructions regarding the right dressings to use, the right cleaning products and the right processes to use twice a day. He said, "Just watch. You will see more and more of those tiny white spots and within time, your leg will soon have all new skin." I began to trust him.

Every day, my daughter interrupted her day to come to take turns with Rick to tend to my wounds. Yes, I said Rick. In the midst of his own bandages and pain, this man took care of me. It was so very painful that I couldn't stand the weight of even the sheet on my legs when I was in bed. This precious man, through his pain and all, built a structure out of PVC pipe so the sheets and blankets could cover me for warmth, but not touch my legs.

Every day, between he and Cari, they would look for those tiny dots to multiply. They could see progress. I wish I could tell you it was quick. It was not.

Much healing takes place in seasons. Be it physical healing, psychological healing, emotional healing, financial healing, and any other kind of healing you can think of. There's a time for every season. There's a greater work that God will do in the process, through the season.

So if you are in a painful "season," be patient. God is moving. God is working. God is using others that you might be blind to in the process. Look for the tiny dots. God will show you that He really is working.

As I shared this with my friend yesterday, it was a real epiphany for him. It's like the light was turned on and he could see that God WAS working. He could feel that there really is a time and season for everything.

Look for the tiny dots. They're there.

Reflection

1. In what ways have you felt like timing was all messed up and things were not coming in to place for you?

2. What kept your mind focused on the struggle so much that you couldn't see God moving?

3. What "tiny dots" might you have looked for that would have helped?

4. Knowing that time stands still for no one, how specifically will you ask God to help you to see the tiny dots in the future?

KEEP WALKING

This morning I was reading in the faith chapter, ***Hebrews 11***. There was such great faith in ordinary people that did extraordinary things. Their faith was securely in their God and not in their circumstances.

There in chapter 11 is a history lesson of faith. From Abel, down through Enoch, Noah, Abraham, Isaac, Jacob, Joseph, Moses and the list goes on of men and women alike. The author said there's not enough time to mention all of them.

I believe that we need a history lesson once in a while. As day-to-day life happens, we all enter into some very dark times. There are situations we face that truly feel like the heavens are like glass and our prayers don't reach God. We wonder where He went or why He's choosing to not respond.

We cry out like the Psalmists in:
Psalm 6:4 NIV *"Turn, Lord, and deliver me; save me because of your unfailing love."*

Psalm 28:2 NIV *"Hear my cry for mercy as I call to you for help."*

Most of us have very little patience during struggles and trials, and wonder where our faith went. We deduce that God is absent and our faith is gone.

> ***We forget that many mountains move one boulder at a time.***

The scriptures tell us that like the saints of old, God gives each of us a measure of faith, and it says that faith is the size of a mustard seed. It goes on to say that this tiny faith is enough to make mountains MOVE. We just expect that they should move quickly. We've all heard testimonies of great mountains in the lives of others that moved quickly. We assume it is always that way. ***We forget that many mountains move one boulder at a time.***

We live in such a drive-thru society that we become extremely anxious in waiting. Even in grocery stores we now have Self-Checkout lanes because we hate to wait. We go to the movies, banks and so many other places that have kiosks so we don't have to wait in long lines to get the things we want. We're all in a hurry, rushing with everything. We become terribly anxious in the "wait."

That anxiousness during struggles and trials leads us to the place where we assume that God has decided to not respond to us for who knows what reason. It's very dark and He's not there. We are anxious, it's dark, and we feel so alone!

Great speaker ***Kyle Dendy said, "Do not mistake the presence of darkness for the absence of God."***

God is there, even in the darkness. God is there, especially IN the darkness.

Think about the Israelites after they left Egypt. They were running for their lives as Pharaoh and his armies were chasing them. If you've seen the old movie ***The 10 Commandments***, you have a clear visual in your head right now.

Hebrews 11:29 NIV *By faith the people passed through the Red Sea as on dry land; but when the Egyptians tried to do so, they were drowned.*

They passed through the Red Sea! The water piled up, and the sea split so they could walk through it to get away from the armies that were after them. Get that picture in your head. The water stacked up around them. Their feet didn't get stuck in the mud, their wagons rolled across like it was dry land. If you think for a minute that they were not terrified, I think you're not thinking clearly. I am certain they were horrified, yet what choice did they have??? God opened up a way for them to get away, and what if it didn't work. What if the waters would crash down and drown them all? Don't you think many of them thought that? This is nuts!!!!! I know I would have. I don't know which would have driven me, my fear or my faith.

What choice did they have but to keep moving? If they froze with fear, they could have sat right down and said "I'm done. This is nuts." They would have drowned with the Egyptians. They could have chosen to **not** step off into the sea to begin with, and would have been taken captive by the Egyptians and likely put to death.

The only choice they had was to keep moving. Just keep moving! Because they were God's children, He protected them. But it was crazy scary, but there was no choice except to keep moving.

I don't know what's piled up around you today. But I do know this: you have to keep moving. Even if you can't see God, He's not left you. He's the one that's holding the waters back so you don't drown. He's the one working on your behalf in ways you could never understand. So we, like the saints of old, must continue to walk in faith. They drew strength through their faith that was the size of a mustard seed.

Scary? Yup! Maybe a little crazy mixed in? Yes! He's working. Trust that. The same as the Israelites trusted Him in the Red Sea. He's splitting the sea for you too! Keep walking!

Reflection

1. What kinds of mountains tend to get in your way?

2. Explain a time when you truly saw a mountain move, one boulder at a time.

3. How did you draw strength from God to wait patiently?

4. How do YOU just keep moving when you feel paralyzed by fear of the waters?

5. How might you encourage someone, practically, to just keep walking?

6. Who can you pray for right now that is in the sea and afraid?

WARDROBE MALFUNCTIONS

What we put on every morning matters, from clothing to attitude. Do we spend as much time every morning thinking about what attitude we will put on, just as we do about our clothing?

The scripture tells us that as Christians there are some things that will show others that we have the Spirit of God living in us. ***Galatians 5*** gives us a list of "fruit" that is displayed in our lives. This is what we should strive to be like every day.

Galatians 5:22-23 NIV says *"But the fruit of the Spirit is love, joy, peace, forbearance, kindness, goodness, faithfulness, gentleness and self-control."*

In our day-to-day life, some fruit are more obviously growing and revealed in us than others. There are days, if we are to be honest, there's some pretty big attitude wardrobe malfunctions for the world to see, or at least those that we live or work with.

One of them that I see missing so often is kindness. I heard someone say: "it costs you absolutely nothing to be kind."

I thought I was a pretty kind person the majority of the time. Well, I discovered recently that my wardrobe didn't include kindness during a particular Sunday morning service.

This lovely lady was sitting two rows ahead of me in church. She came in a few minutes late, as worship was already going on. She scurried in, set her purse and Bible down, and entered in to worship totally oblivious that she had her own wardrobe malfunction going on. She had on a lovely top, with two HUGE tags sticking out the top and back. Right there for the world to see. Some people that are sensitive about their size would die at the thought of their own tags sticking out there, right?

My standard response, in kindness, would have been to simply put my hand on her back, while whispering in her ear that I just tucked in her tag. She would have been grateful. She could have been saved the embarrassment of getting home and realizing that the whole world now knew her size and possibly the maker of her top.

Sounds like a simple thing, right? I've been saved that embarrassment over and over again through the years by the kindness of others. Did I do that for the sister that day? Did I go up, tuck her tag for her? Nope. I sat there wondering why in the world the lady sitting behind her didn't do it. It frustrated me, wondering how in the world the lady in front of me didn't feel it appropriate to save the sister in front of her. I justified my not doing anything by the fact that I was two rows behind her and it would be a disruption for too many if I would get up and do it. Was that truth? I don't know. Just an excuse I think. It was easier to judge someone for not doing it than to just do it myself. God forgive me.

Kindness is really so very simple. Things like that are just being kind. Caring about people and showing kindness is really so very simple. But we excuse ourselves with "well I don't really know her." So now we have to KNOW people to be kind? Or we think "I don't want to embarrass her so I won't draw attention to it." You think she won't be embarrassed when she gets home and realizes it? Or at the end of a long day someone will say, "Hey did you know your tags were hanging out?" You think she wouldn't be embarrassed knowing she walked around like that ALL DAY? All we need to do is be kind. Kindness helps. Kindness shows compassion. Kindness is a simple act focused on the best for someone else.

The fruit of the spirit: kindness. It's really so simple. Ask God to help you show kindness to everyone you come into contact with. I promise you that after my epic fail with the lady and her tag, I asked God to change my heart to be like His. That being kind will always trump any other feeling or justification I may have.

On another note: if you are a guy reading this, ask another lady to tuck in her tags. It's just weird if you do. Also, if you dear sister see a brother with some wardrobe malfunction, ask another dude to deal with it. That's kindness too.

Love and kindness to you all!

Proverbs 14:21 *"...blessed is the one who is kind to the needy."*

Reflection

1. How did you react when you realized you had a spiritual wardrobe malfunction?

2. If fruit grows on a healthy plant, what do you need to do to cultivate good fruit in yourself?

3. How has the simple kindness of someone else affected you?

4. Why is it so hard at times to just be kind?

5. What can you do to remind yourself to keep your eyes and ears open and simply respond to someone else with kindness?

HEART REFLECTIONS

Proverbs 27:19 NLT *As a face is reflected in water, so the heart reflects the real person.*

I have a pastor friend who recently said, "It's easier to look out a window than in a mirror." How much easier it is to look at others and see where they need to change than it is to look at ourselves. Because of that, we can look at these types of scriptures and quickly see flaws in others and never step up to the mirror or look at what our actions reveal about our own heart.

When I look in the mirror, what do I see? The older I'm getting, the more wrinkles and "smile lines" I'm seeing. And some of those "age spots." Yikes, did I actually just say that? Sometimes I put on enough makeup to try to change what I'm seeing. But at the end of the day, it's just me.

Do I give the same diligence to what my actions reveal? The heart reflects the real me. The Word tells us that our hearts are deceitful and wicked, that we can't trust our own hearts. The only solution is a relationship with Jesus Christ. When I enter into relationship with Him, He changes my heart of stone into a soft, pliable one, sensitive to Him. It's only then that every heartbeat will reflect His image. I want others to see Him in me. The question is this: is my heart reflecting the image of the God I serve? What are others seeing in me that can be traced to Him?

There was a story of some ladies that were in a Bible Study, and they were discussing ***Malachi 3:3 NLT*** *"He will sit like a refiner of silver, burning away the dross. He will purify the Levites, refining them like gold and silver, so that they may once again offer acceptable sacrifices to the Lord."*

The big question they had about this scripture was regarding the phrase that the refiner of silver actually sits while the fine metal is in the fire. That sounded strange and they wanted to know more about the process. One of the ladies decided that she would go to a silversmith and ask more questions. During her talk with him, she asked, "Is it true that while the silver is in the fire, that you just sit there?" He said, "Yes, I do." She asked why that was and his response was, "I keep my eye on it so that I don't leave it in too long. It only needs to be in long enough to burn away the impurities. If I left it in too long, it would be destroyed."

She then asked, "Well, how do you know when it's finished?" He replied, "I know it is finished when I am able to see my own reflection in it."

Life isn't random. Bad things don't just happen. We may not know the reason, but we can know this: God is forever working, forever purifying, forever pulling us closer to Him. We are becoming the people He created us to be, reflecting His image. If you're sitting in the fire, know this: He's sitting on the stool and will not take His eye off you. He won't leave you there to destroy you. He loves you enough that you will reflect His image, one of beauty, love, mercy and grace, in the fire, and outside the fire.

He is indeed the great silversmith of our hearts. Do the actions in my life reflect a heart that has been purified? Am I close enough to the silversmith that His work is perfected in my heart?

Proverbs 27:19 NLT *As a face is reflected in water, so the heart reflects the real person.*

What am I reflecting today?

Reflection

1. What do I see when I look in the mirror? (be real here, have some fun)

2. What do YOU think the reflection of your heart reveals?

3. What do those that are close to you see? Ask a couple of people who are close to you and trustworthy.

4. What might you talk to the silversmith about today?

5. Pray that every day, the reflection of your heart would reveal a life that is close to God. Reflect Him today!

WHO BUT GOD?

Proverbs 30:4 NLT *"Who but God goes up to heaven and comes back down? Who holds the wind in his fists? Who wraps up the oceans in his cloak? Who has created the whole wide world? What is his name—and his son's name? Tell me if you know!"*

Who but God can hold the wind in his fists? Who but God wraps up the oceans in his cloak? Who but God has created the whole world? Who? Do you know Him?

This is the God that we serve and the God that we so desperately want others to see, hear and follow. Why? Because He has done cool stuff? Wind in His fists and oceans in His coat? Created the world? Certainly we are amazed by those things. They make us take pause and realize how great He really is. Of course we stop, pause, and praise Him because He is all-mighty. But that's not why we want others to see, hear and follow Him. Because if those are the reasons then we've missed it! If those are the reasons then He's nothing more than a miracle worker. He's nothing more than someone that has amazing powers, kinda like a superhero, but one that we choose to celebrate His birth every year. But why do we?

We see meme's all year long about how many more days before Christmas. Why do we do that? To some it's economical. To others, it is a warm and fuzzy time of year. Yet to others, it's a sad time because they might be celebrating Christmas alone and it's very painful. But what is the reason we celebrate Christmas. If you ask a little one, they will say "Jesus." But what about Him makes us celebrate and want others to know?

- Who but God, who holds the wind in His fists, saw the mess of sin humans were living in and loved us anyway?
- Who but God, out of His great love, made a way for us to have a relationship with Him?
- Who but God, loved us so much that He would send His only Son to come to this earth as an infant, to be born in a cattle stall? 100% human, yet 100% God. That's really hard to grasp. Who but God?
- Who but God, because of His great love for us, showed us the awe and wonder of it all in shepherds and angels gathering on that night to worship that one small child, His Son?
- Who but God, could provide for the financial needs of Mary, Joseph and His Son through some very expensive gifts brought to them by the Wise Men from afar? Wise men that were used by God with great purpose. Read it in ***Matthew 2***. Amazing story!
- Who but God...

In all the craziness of life, we lose the awe and wonder of it all. I had the joy of having Amelia, our young granddaughter for a few hours recently. With all the Christmas stuff up all over the house, she was awe struck. It touched my heart in a new, fresh way. I wiped many tears that day at the sweet, wonder and awe in that dear child. She held the baby Jesus that had been under our tree with such tenderness. She wrapped and unwrapped, and again wrapped and unwrapped Him in the cloth. She kissed Him, hugged Him. She gently laid Him in the little trough. She handled each piece of the manger scene with such care. Then she saw the Santa kneeling at the baby Jesus, worshipping Him. She sat silent, holding them close to her heart. I'm pretty sure Jesus was watching her, smiling at the awe and wonder in that child. She barely spoke as she was caught up in it all. And if you knew her, you would know that is an amazing feat all in itself, just for her to hush.

Have you lost the wonder and awe of it all? Has life taken over and caused you to not see it all quite the same as you once did? My prayer is that this devotion would help you to wrap your heart around the "Who But God" and allow your heart to just breathe, and take it all in. I pray that you are able to focus, if only for a brief moment, on the incredible gift that God has given you in His Son.

Some of you may have lost a loved one this past year, and it has been awful for you. The thought of celebrating a holiday, a birthday or anniversary without that person may be more than you can bear. Let Him wrap His arms around you. Let Him pull you close – so close that you can feel His breath on your neck. He loves you desperately and wants you to trust Him with your pain and loss. For just a moment, breath. For just a moment, visit "Who But God." He will help you focus and celebrate the most precious gift ever – His Son. Through your visit to "Who But God," you will feel His healing ointment deep in your soul. Breathe Him in. No matter who you are. He loves you and has a plan that far exceeds what you can think or imagine. Breathe Him in. There is truly nobody like Him. And He wants to spend today, tomorrow, and every tomorrow with you. That brings incredible awe and wonder. Just breathe.

Reflection

1. What about the greatness of God gives you pause?

2. *"Who holds the wind in his fists? Who wraps up the oceans in his cloak?"* These are some pretty descriptive word pictures. What questions or thoughts do they bring to your mind?

3. What life situations do you have right now that are stressful, painful or uncertain?

4. How does the "Who But God" scriptures help you to trust that He cares about you?

Prayer:
Father God, help me to trust You today. No matter how difficult or stressful, regardless of how painful or uncertain, I choose to trust You. Help me to look to Your Word, stand on Your promises, and just breathe You in. Help me to grasp just how wide, how deep and how great Your love is for me. Help me to just breathe You in. In Jesus Name...Amen.

WHO'S AT THE TABLE?

Hebrews 13:15-16 NIV *Through Jesus, therefore, let us continually offer to God a sacrifice of praise — the fruit of lips that confess his name.* [16] *And do not forget to do good and to share with others, for with such sacrifices God is pleased.*

Do you cook Thanksgiving dinner? Do you spend it with others that graciously invite you to their home for dinner? Do you go out instead of cook? Do you spend it alone, no family or friends close?

There's nothing like the traditional Thanksgiving feast: turkey, stuffing, mashed potatoes, yams, cranberry sauce, that famous green bean casserole, corn, Brussels sprouts, and???? Awesome meal that is always better spent with people you care about. Even peanut butter and jelly tastes better with someone you care about.

There has been a tradition in the Ganiere family for as long as we've been married. If we find someone that has nowhere to go for dinner, our table is open. We make room. Please don't start sending in your reservations for this year. That's seriously a concern when I say stuff like this. ☺

Our children, all adults now, know they are welcome to invite someone they find out is alone on that holiday. They let me know, and we make room. Not just for dinner, but in our hearts. Don't feel bad for someone that's alone if you're not willing to open your table and your heart.

I am well aware of how risky it is to invite people into THIS family. We laugh until our sides hurt, eat WAY too much food, and some fall into a turkey coma before dessert. I can't tell you that the conversation is always ready for "prime time." We're family, and there's not a lot of rules about what topics can come up. To some guests I have apologized for the craziness in our house. You know what? People have always said, "Your family is real. I feel so comfortable."

I said all that to say: don't spend Thanksgiving dinner alone. In fact, there are many dinners that this could apply to. The Word makes it clear that we are to *"do good and to share with others, for with such sacrifices God is pleased."* So who's gonna be at YOUR table? Take a risk and invite someone you know is alone. In taking the risk, you just might make a good friend.

Earlier I mentioned sharing peanut butter and jelly with someone. I mean it. If you can't afford a dinner, invite them over to share what you DO have. Again, I can hear it: who's gonna wanna eat PB and J for Thanksgiving? Well, YOU, if that is all you've got. Share what you have. How fun would it be, and all the giggles that come with it to light a candle and share a PB & J with a friend. Remember the Word says: *"do good and to share with others, for with such sacrifices God is pleased."* Even if it's PB & J. So who's gonna be at your table? Thanksgiving or any other time that you just may not want to be alone.

One more thought: surely someone reading this is saying, "I'm going to someone else's house, I can't invite someone along." Who says you can't? If God points out someone to you that will be alone, call your host or hostess and ask if you could bring someone along that will be alone that day. If the answer is "sorry, no room," thank them and make plans to get together with your friend later, or earlier. That way, you won't "diss" your family, but can still spend some time with the one that's alone.

I could go on and on and on about this. Our family has had very few Thanksgiving dinners where we didn't have someone else, or several other people with us. It has enriched our family. So who do you know that will be alone – Thanksgiving, a birthday or other holiday? What a blessing you can be. God is pleased when we share with others.

Reflection

I have gotten so much kick back from people over the years about this. Seriously. My heart is saddened at the fear or selfishness that stops people from bringing others in to family celebrations. I've also talked to so many that were just plain sad that they had to spend a holiday alone. WHY??? This goes both ways. If you're the one alone – do something about it. Be a blessing to someone else. That is a sacrifice that is pleasing to God.

1. What holiday is coming up that you could create an environment to be a blessing to someone else?

2. If inviting someone to your home is a problem for you, ask yourself "why?" Be honest with yourself and God and come to grips with the truth of why this is hard for you.

3. If you simply don't have the ways and means to do it, where else could you ask someone else to meet you so that neither of you is alone? Think out of the box.

4. *"And do not forget to do good and to share with others, for with such sacrifices God is pleased."* Mark it down now. What can you do to sacrifice for someone else?

5. Then, make a plan and do it!

PENGUIN PRINCIPLE ONE

I saw the movie, ***March of the Penguins,*** in 2005 on a flight from Milwaukee, WI to Quepos, Costa Rica, to do missions work. I was so inspired by the purpose and instincts of those penguins. They are so determined to accomplish their purpose, that little to nothing could stop them. I saw some correlations between those penguins and humans in relationship to each other.

In the interest of a short devotion, I can't possibly share all I learned from those little penguins. I share in much more detail in my book ***This Pyramid***. But I do want to touch on a couple of those principles, today and tomorrow. The first one is:

Instinct, Inner Compass or GPS
In the movie, ***March of the Penguins***, Morgan Freeman said that penguins' instinct is like "**an invisible compass.**" They just know where to go. They just know what to do. *"Their destination is always the same, but the terrain is not."* They just know. There's an innate impulse and natural aptitude they all have which is called instinct!

Think with me for a minute. As Christians, we have the incredible Spirit of God that lives inside of us, giving us truth, giving us the words to say when we have none, telling us what to say, where to go and when. We have the choice every day to follow the Spirit or ignore His voice.

Luke 12:12 NIV *"the Holy Spirit will teach you at that time what you should say."*

John 16:13 NIV *"But when he, the Spirit of truth, comes, he will guide you into all truth. He will not speak on his own; he will speak only what he hears, and he will tell you what is yet to come."*

As Christians we have in inner compass in the Holy Spirit. It is our choice if we will follow or not.

The Holy Spirit won't MAKE us go in the right direction, but He will show us the way to go. God loved us too much to expect us to hopefully find or stay on the path every day. His Holy Spirit leads, guides, directs, and lets us know when we're on course and when we're off course. Much like the instinct of those little penguins.

I've lived in the Greater Milwaukee area all of my life. I know this town like the back of my hand. But get me out of town, and I can lose my way pretty quick. I'm also an optimist by nature, so I never say "I'm lost," I just got off track. I'm also a biker, meaning that in riding my Harley it is always about the journey, so everything becomes an adventure. The adventure can be dangerous when you don't rely on the Holy Spirit to help you be where you need to be in life.

In my car, I have a GPS that I call Lola. Lola is awesome. She tells me which way to turn, and how far I need to go, and will even tell me the approximate arrival time – **IF** I follow her directions. Sometimes she shows me off-roading, but she always knows where I am.

Lola will also re-calculate over and over if I refuse to follow her lead. You know how it is; sometimes we just know a short cut and bypass what Lola says. She doesn't get confused. She just re-calculates. I love Lola. If I mess up, she'll get me back on track, IF I listen to what she says.

How often do we treat the Holy Spirit like we do our GPS? If we get stuck, we really rely on His direction. Otherwise we just try to navigate ourselves. When we "off road," the Holy Spirit tries to tell us much like my Lola: "Re-calculating...make a u-turn at the next available opportunity...turn left at the corner and...Re-calculating." Sometimes we listen, sometimes we don't.

Good thing I'm not Lola. I'd get ticked with me and just give up trying to correct my choice of path. I'd let the windshield grip loosen and just go crashing to the floor of my car. "You don't listen anyway, why do I try? Stupid human!"

The Holy Spirit of God is so much more than an inner compass or GPS. He takes up residence inside us when we accept Jesus as our Lord and Savior. He gives us this inner compass to teach, to lead, to guide, to convict us of sin. Sometimes we listen, sometimes we off-road, or go our own short cut. Those short cuts often turn out to be LONG cuts because we should have listened to the Spirit the first time around.

Our willingness to listen to the Spirit is directly connected to the depth of our relationship with God. Do I spend time with the one I love every day? Do I seek His instruction? Do I listen to His voice? Do I do what He tells me to do or try to short cut it?

Our willingness to listen to the Spirit is directly connected to the depth of our relationship with God.

A heart that desires to follow Him every day will pray for wisdom and direction knowing that in His Spirit is the path that leads to life.

Psalm 25:4-5 NIV *"Show me your ways, O LORD, teach me your paths; guide me in your truth and teach me, for you are God my Savior, and my hope is in you all day long."*

Proverbs 4:10-13 NIV *"Listen, my son, accept what I say, and the years of your life will be many. I guide you in the way of wisdom and lead you along straight paths. When you walk, your steps will not be hampered; when you run, you will not stumble. Hold on to instruction; do not let it go; guard it well, for it is your life."*

Father, give us ears to hear. You've given us your precious Holy Spirit. Let us hear Him every day and walk in the abundance of the life that You have for us. That is where our protection is, our safety, wisdom and instructions are. Give us ears to hear.

Reflection

1. When was it that you realized that as a Christian you had the Holy Spirit as your inner compass?

2. Explain the joys of following the Spirit in day-to-day life.

3. In what areas of your life do you find yourself not listening to the Holy Spirit?

4. What excuses do you tend to make for "off-roading?"

5. What can you do every day to make sure you have your Holy Spirit GPS on?

PENGUIN PRINCIPLE TWO

There is so much more than I could ever cover here about these amazing penguins. Do some research and watch the movie. You will be amazed at the similarities we can draw to our everyday lives.

Just some facts about those penguins:

- They instinctively know that **they need each other.**
- **They depend on each other.**
- **They fight for each other.**
- **They sacrifice and sometimes go without** so that their family can survive.
- **They band together during storms** and instinctively know to protect each other.
- **They work together.**

Instinctively these little penguins know they need each other. They depend on each other and take care of each other. They see storms coming and band together to weather the storms because it's just not ok for one of them to not survive.

I worry about us as the church. Do we realize how much we need each other? Are we willing to fight for each other's safety? Will we sacrifice for one another and give up a comfort so someone else can survive, physically or spiritually? Will we pull together to be sure we're all safe? That requires working together. Will we?

Winter Survival

Penguins endure horrible arctic winters. The dads and the chicks, along with the rest in the colony, protect each other while they await nourishment to arrive. The females have gone on a journey to the ocean to get food. The others huddle together to survive while she's gone. Survival in the arctic winters isn't possible alone. They realize they need each other if they are going to make it, and more importantly, that the young chicks will make it.

To weather the storms of winter, they gather together forming a big circle with everyone in their colony coming together. They each find a secure spot somewhere in that circle, fitting everyone in tightly, so that no one is out there alone, freezing. They are not concerned where they are in that huddle, because they know they take care of each other. They don't fight for the best spot because they will each have a time in the cold as a barrier to protect the others, followed by a time in the warmth so they themselves don't freeze to death.

In a large circle of bodies, there are some on the inside of the huddle, the warmest place to be. There are also some on the outside of the huddle, the coldest place to be. They live every moment constantly shuffling, moving, slowly, rotating in complete unity in that circle. Working together, they all move slowly, in the same direction, everyone in survival mode, that none would be lost. If they don't, some would freeze to death and the loss of life is just unacceptable to the colony. So, together they survive the worst arctic weather.

I have watched that documentary numerous times. Each time, I couldn't help but wonder how we, God's people, the Body of Christ, respond to each other during difficult times as well as day-to-day life.

- Do we pull together in the good times as well as the bad?
- Do we argue about the best solutions to end the crisis?
- Do we push some away if they don't participate the way we think they should?
- Do we allow our circumstances to draw us together or do we use them to tear us apart?
- Do we sacrifice ourselves for the sake of another?

We have been through some extremely difficult crisis in church throughout the years. Some have drawn us together, and sadly, others have torn us apart. We pick sides like the world picks sides in an election or on a baseball or football team. We slam the other side; we trash talk like the world does when they disagree with a method or path.

I can tell you from experience; the times that brought incredible healing are the times that we drew together. When we chose to be tight, all for one and one for all, pulling together for the good of us all. Even, no especially, when we didn't agree. We were the body of Christ.

Do I see you as more important than me? Am I fighting for myself, and only thinking about MY good? To you, dear friend, are others a priority to you? Or are you focused on yourself?

In our biological family, we have used a well-used phrase when crisis hits: we're blood. We are family with common blood running through our veins. We do what is the best for "US."

Body of Christ, Church, we also have the blood of Christ coursing through our veins, binding us tight as His Body. We are blood. Our focus should be on "us," and not selfishly focused on ourselves. That's what "blood" does.

Will we, the Church, deal with crisis the same - with day-to-day life together? The blessing and favor of God rests on us as a whole when we choose to live together in unity – we are blood. First and foremost, we are family.

I John 2:7 NIV *"Dear friends, I am not writing a new commandment for you; rather it is an old one you have had from the very beginning. This old commandment—to love one another—is the same message you heard before."*

There are so many more scriptures that talk about the body and our love for each other. These are just a few:

I Corinthians 12; I Corinthians 13; John 13:35; Romans 13:8; Galatians 5:18; I Thessalonians 3:12; I Thessalonians 4:9; II Thessalonians 1:3; Hebrews 10:24; I John 3:11; I John 3:23; I John 4:7 & 8; II John 1:5 & 8

Reflection

1. What was your take away from this devotion?

2. In what ways do you think you can better connect to the body of Christ?

3. Share an example of a meaningful time when the body of Christ was there for you during a difficult time. How did it help you?

4. Who can you reach out to so that they too are kept safe as they are facing a storm?

5. What struggle might you be going through right now that you need the body to be there for you? Will you tell them?

CLOSING THOUGHTS

One of the greatest tragedies I've seen over the years is for someone to go through a crisis alone. They were not connected very well to the body of Christ, and no one knew. Many times, they got angry because the "church" wasn't there for them. But no one knew.

If that's you, and you have been hurt, please know that God does care. There is a good chance that His people didn't know, weren't listening, or maybe in your hurt, you pulled away. I will stand in for those and say to you, "I'm so very sorry. You should not have had to walk alone. Please forgive us. We can and will do better in Jesus Name."

If you are not connected to a good church, please email us and we will be happy to help you find a good, loving church, where people truly love and care for people. You can email us at resourcemin@gmail.com.

God bless you friends. As you follow Him and walk in obedience to His Word, His incredible blessings will rest on you all the days of your lives.

Working the Seeds, page 25

Jeremiah, D. (2009) *Living with Confidence in a Chaotic World.* Nashville, TN: Thomas Nelson, Inc.

Are You Ready?, page 37-38

LaHaye, T. Jenkins, J. (1995-2007) *Left Behind* (Books 1-16). Wheaton, IL: Tyndale House.

Put Some "Extra" in Your Ordinary, page 43

Furtick, S. (2010) *Sun Stand Still: What Happens When You Dare to Ask God for the Impossible.* Colorado Springs, CO: Multnomah Books.

Faith Squasher No. 2 - Comparison, page 54

Madu, R. (New Life). (2014, August 14). *Running the Race God Has Set Before Us* [Video podcast]. Retrieved from www.theleadershipcollective.org.

Faith Squasher No. 2 - Comparison, page 55

Groeschel, C. (2015) *#Struggles: Following Jesus in a Selfie-Centered World.* Grand Rapids, MI: Zondervan.

Faith Squasher No. 4 - Unforgiveness, page 64

Mayo, J. (2014, November 21). *Trying to be EVERYTHING for Everyone?* [Blog]. Retrieved from jeannemayo.com/blog.

Redeem the Time, page 75
Boom, C.T., Sherrill, J. L. & Sherrill, E. (1974) *The Hiding Place: the Triumphant True Story of Corrie Ten Boom.* New York, NY: Bantam.

Do Good, page 78
Carson, B. & Murphey, C. (2010) *Gifted Hands: the Ben Carson Story.* Grand Rapids, MI: Zondervan.

The End is in Sight, page 85
Butcher, S. (1982) *The End Is in Sight.* Precious Moments, Jonathan and David.

Company Loyalties and Labels, page 90
Stark, R. (Producer), & Ross, H (Director). (1989). *Steel Magnolias* [Motion picture]. United States: TriStar Pictures.

It's a Trap, page 103
Kendrick, A. & Kendrick, S. (Producers), & Kendrick, A. (Director). (2015). *War Room* [Motion picture]. United States: Sony Pictures Home Entertainment.

Kendrick, S. (2015) *War Room: Bible Study.* Nashville, TN: LifeWayPress.

Trust in the Lord, page 117
Butcher, S. (1984) *Trust in the Lord to the Finish.* Precious Moments, Jonathan and David.

Keep Walking, page 124
Dendy, K. [Kyle Dendy]. (2016, September 26). *Do Not Mistake the Presence of Darkness for the Absence of God* [Video file].

Penguin Principle One, page 143
Darondeau, Y., Lioud, C. & Priou, E. (Producers), & Jacquet, L. (Director). (2005). *March of the Penguins* [Motion picture]. United States: Warner Home Movie.

Made in the USA
Middletown, DE
05 April 2022

63652838R00089